HUMAN ACHIEVEMENT
AND DIVINE VOCATION IN
THE MESSAGE OF PAUL

STUDIES IN BIBLICAL THEOLOGY

HUMAN ACHIEVEMENT AND DIVINE VOCATION IN THE MESSAGE OF PAUL

WILLIAM A. BEARDSLEE

ALEC R. ALLENSON, INC.
635 EAST OGDEN AVENUE
NAPERVILLE, ILL.

FIRST PUBLISHED 1961
PRINTED IN GREAT BRITAIN BY
W. & J. MACKAY & CO LTD
CHATHAM

CONTENTS

PREFACE

THE central problem of Pauline studies is the recovery of the meaning of justification by faith. Easily lost or legalized, this base of Pauline faith must be newly perceived in each new situation of the Church. Penetrating studies of Paul in our own time have grappled with this central issue from various points of view, and have done much to make the meaning of Pauline faith accessible to our time. The present study is concerned to explore an aspect of Paul's thought which is often overlooked—his intense concern for human achievement. It attempts to indicate some implications which Paul's insights may have for contemporary Christian theology, and to set forth in Paul's own terms his high sense of the work to which man may be called by God. To Paul it appeared that the achievements of the apostle or the believer were not set over against justification by faith, but were rather the fruit of the same divine purpose which is met in God's forgiveness. Thus the theme of this study is not to be set in opposition to the central Pauline theme of justification but is to be seen as a consequence or complement.

The author is indebted not only to the many scholars whose work can be only inadequately acknowledged in the notes, but also particularly to his father, and to Professor Amos N. Wilder, under whose guidance an earlier study of the topic was prepared as a dissertation at the University of Chicago, as well as to several colleagues and former colleagues at Emory University. He also desires to express his appreciation of two grants by the Emory University Research Committee and to thank Mrs Martha McKay for the preparation of the indexes.

W. A. BEARDSLEE

Emory University
June, 1960

7

ABBREVIATIONS

Beginnings: *The Beginnings of Christianity*, ed. F. J. Foakes Jackson
and Kirsopp Lake. Part 1, The Acts of the Apostles, vols.
I–V, 1920–33
CNT: Commentaire du Nouveau Testament
ET: English translation
HNT: Handbuch zum Neuen Testament, ed. H. Lietzmann
HTR: *Harvard Theological Review*
ICC: International Critical Commentary
JBL: *Journal of Biblical Literature*
MNTC: Moffatt New Testament Commentary
RHPR: *Revue d'Histoire et de Philosophie religieuses*
Sanday and Headlam: W. Sanday and A. C. Headlam, *Romans*
(ICC), London, 1895
SBT: Studies in Biblical Theology
TWNT: *Theologisches Wörterbuch zum Neuen Testament*
Weiss: J. Weiss, *The History of Primitive Christianity* (completed
. . . by Rudolf Knopf), trans. by four friends and ed. by F. C.
Grant, London, 1937

Note: With exceptions usually noted, the Bible is cited in the
Revised Standard Version.

I

INTRODUCTION

THIS book is a study of Paul's understanding of divine vocation and of the way in which the divine call may use and fulfil the human striving for achievement which can only be frustrated unless it becomes a response to God's call. Paul's understanding of himself and of his own task provides the clearest example of his message about vocation and achievement generally. He had a deep awareness of the precariousness and impotence of human existence, when it is cut off from the deeper sources of its life. But he also expressed a clear and robust confidence that once the structures of man's life had been renewed by the goodness of God, the 'goal-directed' impulses of human life may really be fulfilled, precisely by the fact that God may choose to use a man or a community in the achievement of his own life-renewing purpose. Paul's perspective is conceived at all points in a strictly Christological frame of reference. God's action in Christ is the one channel through which the renewing powers become available and will become available to men. Paul finds his high understanding of his own work and achievement as 'apostle of Christ' by finding himself in a situation of ultimate crisis, in which the confrontation with Christ means not only encountering a power that severs his dependence on the powers of 'this world' within and around him, but also means being drawn into a critical task at the crucial turning-point of the history of God's purpose.

Impressive as is Paul's own sense of vocation, he does not understand it as an individual experience. His task is given in the context of the community of Christ. The whole Church shares in the calling to represent Christ and work for him. Paul thus understands the Church to be an unique community, which finds its order and goal in God's 'history', yet exits for the moment in man's history apparently like any other group. The Church is both like and unlike other 'historical' communities—like, in that it is constituted by the interaction of continuing personal histories, and has continuity in time; unlike, in that it derives its energies from Christ, and is not dependent for its existence and growth on the power-structures around it.

This study will examine Paul's understanding of 'history', the overall setting within which the self is called to work, and will then turn to an examination of Paul's view of work, progress, the apostolate, the slave and servant of God, and the work of Christ in comparison with the work of the chosen man. The central theme of these specific studies will be the calling of man by God through Christ and the response of man in obedience and work. Before turning to these studies, we shall indicate some of the ways in which a more exact assessment of the 'vocation and work' aspect of Paul's thought may be significant for contemporary Protestant theology. For the situation in contemporary theological discussion is one in which interpreters have been able to present the Pauline understanding of faith in vital and relevant ways, but have found it more difficult to make use of Paul's grasp of the meaning for faith of vocation and work.

FAITH AND CULTURE

One reason for the comparative neglect of Paul's thought about vocation and work is that those who deal with the themes of vocation and work most frequently approach them from the point of view of their meaning in culture. The crisis of Western culture in which we find ourselves has aroused new interest in developing a theology of culture, and yet Paul's way of understanding work has little immediate relevance to the problems of culture. For Paul does not think of Christ as calling men to find meaning in or to renew the vitality of that pattern of human tradition and life which we call 'culture'. The social, intellectual, moral, and aesthetic forms which constitute culture were for him primarily manifestations of the 'wisdom of this world', and stood in opposition to the new life given by Christ. The note of judgment is hence the primary thrust of Paul's message in relation to culture. For him, men cannot find life through culture, or through its enrichment or renewal. Not only individual loyalties, but all the interlocking structures of power and of standards and values stand under the condemnation of God. Paul's turning from the 'wisdom of this world' to a new all-embracing loyalty to Christ involves a renunciation of confidence in culture, and shows that cultural goals cannot be directly derived from Paul's kind of faith.

None the less, a confrontation with Paul can be a fruitful part of the dialogue exploring the relation between faith and culture. The very sharpness of God's judgment on cultural achievement, as seen in the message of Paul, must be the central and initial note of any statement of a biblical theology of culture. Christian faith makes men aliens to the culture in which they live, and gives them a freedom from dependence upon its standards and its powers, the reaffirmation of which is a primary task of Christian thinkers, particularly in our situation, in which Christianity has become so deeply involved in Western culture that it is in danger of losing its power to stand over against its environing culture in judgment.

A second note in Paul's message, though a subsidiary one, is also important. Paul's concern for expressing faith and love in a community re-enlists many of the cultural energies which are discarded as prime goals. To cite one small but revealing example, Paul's reinvigoration of Greek rhetoric has often been noticed.[1] To Paul his literary achievement seems to have been largely an unnoticed side-effect of his activity, but it is a solid instance of the way in which his view of vocation and work may have an unexpected culture-renewing function. Paul's thought cannot provide a base from which to justify Christianity as something which might 'save civilization'. It can, however, suggest the possibility that work done for other than cultural goals may also set free forces which will, incidentally to their conscious purpose, effect a partial renewal of the patterns of cultural activity. The contribution of Paul's message to this aspect of the discussion of faith and culture will be to present a way of understanding Christian faith which involves a separating of the self from dependence on 'this world', yet one which does not leave the self isolated for the moment of faith. Rather, it sees the self brought into a community which is turned toward God as known in Christ, and in which the

[1] Cf. Edouard Norden, *Die antike Kunstprosa* (5th [reprinted] ed.) Darmstadt, 1958, II, p. 459 (on I Cor. 13).

will of God in Christ draws it toward a life of spontaneous obedience to God, and of unreserved openness to one another. Patterns of activity from the environing culture which can be used or modified to express this vision will be used and reshaped by the community of faith. If cultural patterns cannot be so understood, they will be rejected. A further exploration of the relevance of such a vision of the Christian's and the Church's task to the crisis of culture can be an important phase of contemporary theological inquiry.

MAN AND GOD

The apparent irrelevance of Paul's understanding of vocation, for Christians who are in fact far more deeply committed to their culture than was Paul, is one reason for lack of attention to his understanding of work and achievement. An equally important reason is that contemporary theology finds it far easier to speak with integrity and authenticity about man and his response of faith than about God and his purpose. For Paul, on the other hand, vocation and work are grounded in an understanding of God's will, so that although his message about work may seem to reflect a new pre-occupation with human effort, it is really based on a profound faith in God's purpose. It is difficult for the modern thinker to speak about God, for traditional theological language has been pervasively shaped by idealistic categories of thought which are now increasingly thought to be inadequate to represent reality. Contemporary categories provide alternatives that seem more adequate to represent the reality of the world, but are not obviously suited to speak of the transcendent. Thus the technical question of the nature and scope of theological language has come sharply into focus, and is leading to a significant rediscovery of biblical thought as dynamic and functional rather than substantial and idealist. Biblical categories are welcomed theologically not only as more adequate for expressing the reality with which the biblical message deals, than were many of the more idealistic categories of traditional theology, but also as more suitable for the communication of the gospel to a world which is rejecting the reality of an 'other world' idealistically conceived.

The rejection of the ideal transcendent world, however, springs from a deeper source than the obsolescence of a traditional set of theological categories. An important part of the history of the modern West is the history of a gradual loss or weakening of the awareness of the holy. Today the emptiness of much traditional religion as well as the void disclosed in so much contemporary creative art and writing testifies to the lack of awareness of the holy in our time. The Jewish theologian Martin Buber speaks of the 'eclipse of God' in the modern West.[1] Christian thinkers recognize and confront the 'absence of God' in various ways; the turning away from 'natural theology' is one example, while the concentration on man's response of faith, rather than on God, is another. Consciousness of this erosion of awareness of the holy has compelled the Christian thinker to try to think more clearly about the difference between religion and Christian faith, and in particular has made him sensitive to the danger of making the God who is known into an idol. None the less, it is a striking charac-teristic of much of the most sensitive and thoughtful interpretation of the Christian faith in our time that it is balanced heavily on the side of the human response of faith, and is very hesitant to make affirmations about the God to whom faith responds. Precisely in this situation of contemporary interpretation it will be important to turn to Paul's understanding of vocation. For Paul is the great model for Christian thinking about faith as unreserved openness to God in Christ, and as renunciation of all claim to justify oneself before God. Yet his profound and gripping message about the human response of faith includes a real apprehension of God and his purposes. Neither God nor the structure of divine action is seen objectively, but rather both are viewed in encounter and in the deepest personal participation. Paul's view of vocation, then, finds its deepest theological significance not in a fuller view of human response (as over against a view of faith which overlooked the dimension of vocation and work), but in a fuller apprehension of the divine purpose made known in Christ, which is able to call and use men. Theology can most fruitfully press beyond the analysis of faith to affirmations about God precisely through study of the purpose of God for men, a study which involves relating New Testament eschatology to the life and thought of today. Adequate theological interpretation demands affirmations which will avoid the danger of speaking of God in such a way that he

[1]Martin Buber, *Eclipse of God*, London, 1953.

is put at man's disposal, while yet presenting Christian faith as a gospel, a proclamation that God in Christ has broken the powers of evil.

ESCHATOLOGY

Paul understands his vocation in eschatological terms, finding his own place and work in the culminating process of a divine purpose which will destroy the structures of power in which men live. The interpreter must relate Paul's eschatological vision to the contemporary situation of man and the Church.

The simplest form of adaptation is to affirm that during the 'time of the Church' the eschatological process has stopped temporarily, to be resumed at the final end. In effect this has been the view of traditional Protestant theology. Such a view provides a way of integrating later, less eschatological Christianity with its early eschatological beginnings. It rightly suggests that faith does not expect all times to be presented with the same possibilities. It implies that just as the divine purpose is not uniformly manifested in man's life, but encounters him in certain decisive crises, so too the possibility of complete detachment from the powers of this world is not uniformly present even in the community of faith. There is much truth in the admission that the possibilities of faith are limited by the times in which one lives. The unbreakable bond by which Paul was united not simply to the living Christ but uniquely to the resurrected Lord is a reminder that his self-understanding sprang from a unique situation, and must always remain in part inaccessible to the modern believer. Indeed, the dying-out of the apostolate in the early Church is a witness to the fact that emerging Christianity itself recognized that such a peak of self-awareness before God could not be perpetuated in the Church. It would be impossible to suggest that Paul should become a model for all Christian thinking about vocation.

On the other hand, the attempt to interpret eschatology to the contemporary Church simply by extending its temporal framework is inadequate, and indeed in effect de-eschatologizes the Christian message. For early Christian eschatology was not only a confrontation of the individual 'will' with alternatives of ultimate destiny, but a confrontation of the whole structure of man's life in the world, and the proclamation of a gospel which claimed to set men free from that structure to live—if only in anticipation—by the powers of the new age.

Many contemporary interpreters are rightly cautious about adopting the objective structure of the ancient eschatological vision into their thought. More than by the remoteness of this ancient form of thought, they are deterred by the fear that too clear a picture of the ultimate outcome may deprive men of the necessity of facing up to the radical decision of faith. Such thinkers find the relevance of eschatology in the total claim of faith with which it confronts the believer. They rightly see that the primary impact of New Testament faith is its demand for a reversal of the standards of this world and for a willingness to be rejected by those who are judged successful in it. Yet from just this point of view it should be possible to see in Paul's self-understanding a legitimate way of moving beyond the moment of self-renunciation and faith to the continuing life of responsible love in the community of faith.

Paul's bold faith that he was an 'eschatological participant' was based on the conviction that God and his purposes were really, if imperfectly, known. A confidence like Paul's that one's work can have meaning in the context of the divine purpose, cannot exist in any real sense apart from some understanding of what the divine purpose is. Thus we should affirm that even though the New Testament presents God's purpose in eschatological language, in which modern men can no longer completely share, none the less the vision of the victory of God's goodness is an indispensable base for Christian thought. As an instance we may cite Rom. 11, a chapter which will play a considerable part in the discussion of apostleship.[1] A recent writer attacks the theology of history which Paul unfolds in this chapter, to the extent that it presents a view of the future, as 'theologically illegitimate'.[2] One may agree that in so far as Rom. 11 represents a speculative picture of future events it is of secondary importance, but as an expression of faith in the purpose of God it remains central not only for the interpretation of Paul's thought historically, but also for the

[1]See ch. V.
[2]Erich Dinkler, 'Earliest Christianity', in *The Idea of History in the Ancient Near East*, ed. R. C. Dentan, New Haven, 1955, p. 185.

consideration of his relevance today. That some details cannot be pressed as visible human history is unimportant, as in the parallel case of certain 'unfulfilled' Old Testament prophecies.[1] The importance of Rom. 11 is that it brings a vision of the over-arching bounty of God's purpose into relevant connexion with the seeming limitation of his goodness involved in the rejection of Christ by his own people. While the modern theologian cannot simply accept the predictive details of Rom. 11, he must strive to deal adequately with the faith that God's unmeasurable goodness will ultimately be made effective in relation to the structures of human community in time. Despite the justified fear of 'otherworldliness', the resurrection as an aspect of eschatological faith requires more central attention than it often receives. As the fulfilment of the vision of the whole existence of man made new in the presence of God, the resurrection is essential for the kind of faith in the divine purpose which Paul manifests.[2] It is true that much of the most perceptive work of Christian thought and sensitivity in our time is pointed toward bringing out the lostness of man and the 'absence of God' from structures and experiences which were once seen as manifestations of God. None the less, the serious quest for relevant ways of affirming the ultimate goodness of God does not represent a turning away from identification with the tragic agony of our time, but an embracing of it and ministering in it.

THE CHURCH

Another area of theological relevance is Paul's understanding of the Church, the context within which he perceived his vocation. The single-mindedness of Paul's devotion to his task is grounded in his conviction that the community in which he is called has access to a power of a different order from that available in other societies. For him the radical break between 'Church' and 'world' was perceived in an eschatological context. As the sense of participation in a crisis of divine action was lost by succeeding

---

[1] E.g., the prophecies of the restoration of the Northern Kingdom in Jer. 31.2–6, 16–20, which likewise spring from a faith in God's purpose which remains relevant even though the events prophesied did not take place.

[2] Cf. J. A. T. Robinson, *The Body: A Study in Pauline Theology* (SBT 5), London, 1952, pp. 82 ff.

generations, the more static forms in which the divine presence
was expressed came more and more to partake of a striking similarity to the powers effective in other communities. The churches
of our time are so deeply involved in the culture in which they
live that it is hard for us to claim honestly that they are the
eschatological community, set apart from the world by an act of
even cosmic significance, of which Paul writes. Once again, as
in the question of culture, the primary impact of Paul's message is
to set before the Church God's judgment on its failure. The
Church is not intended to identify itself so easily with the world
in which it lives, and it cannot find the positive meaning of
Paul's thought until it has listened seriously to the word of
judgment.

But Paul's understanding of the Church as the context of
continuing work can also be a fruitful line to explore in moving
through and beyond the note of judgment. In his view of work,
obedience to Christ is the only factor that gives work any enduring
or ultimate meaning, and this obedience, specified by the figure
of Christ himself, has the content of self-denying love and is
oriented toward the confrontation of God and toward the vision
of a society of men freely giving of themselves to each other.
Such a vision of obedience nullifies the absolute worth of all
other patterns of life, yet within the new community some patterns
previously followed continue, since they can be vehicles through
which the new purpose is expressed.[1] In particular, work continues
much as before. In contrast to the Qumran community, Paul
refused to set up an external form appropriate to 'sacred' work.[2]
The old work takes on a new significance. Since it is informed by
the new Spirit, it is seen in an entirely new structure, and it can
serve concrete ends in the new community. Paul opposes the
tendency to set up specific patterns of 'Christian' work. Instead
he insists that only as a man's activities are authentically directed
toward the distinctive goals of Christ are they real work, and if
they are so directed, many of the traditional activities can be

[1]That the acceptance of some previously-established patterns does not
imply a mere quietist acceptance of 'the world' is well brought out by Amos
N. Wilder, 'Kerygma, eschatology, and social ethics', in *The Background of
the New Testament and Its Eschatology,* ed. W. D. Davies and D. Daube,
Cambridge, 1956, pp. 509–36.
[2]See ch. III.

taken up into the new pattern of obedience. In the new setting for work, concrete tasks can be undertaken with wholehearted devotion, even though in any specific case the effort may come to nothing. In so far as they participate in the new Spirit, such tasks are believed to find their real fulfilment in the new age which God will establish. Thus the life of the Church is a setting within which obedience to Christ is seen in more than individualistic (pietistic or existentialist) terms; it becomes a context within which the structures of power and custom can be evaluated and used with freedom for the purpose of *agapē*, and it is a setting within which faith in God's power in Christ sets the believer free from anxiety about the permanence of his achievements. Ephemeral and fragile as the tenderness toward the weak brother may seem, he knows it to be an expression of the purpose of God himself.

As such themes are explored, the theologian must recognize that in the modern situation the boundary between the Church and the world has become so blunted that the themes of encounter with the mystery of judgment and of ultimate holy goodness, and of finding all one's energies enlisted in response and work which have the quality of tenderness, cannot be claimed as the property of any one objectively definable group. Some who stand outside the formal boundaries of the Church may be more honest witnesses to the posture of faith and to the reality of God than the conventional Christian. Such a recognition need not entail the abandonment of the Christocentric orientation which is so central for Paul, but it will demand the recognition that the encounter with the reality which the Christian knows as Christ may be found about him under names which he may not at once recognize.

VOCATION

Finally, Paul's view of vocation itself must be considered by the theologian. Paul believed himself to be 'a man who has been appointed to a proper place and a peculiar task in the series of events to be accomplished in the final days of this world'.[1] Like many others of the 'prophetic-puritan' type to which he belongs, Paul shows both a striking unconcern for the problems of 'culture'

[1]Anton Fridrichsen, 'The Apostle and his message', *Uppsala Universitets Aarsskrift* (1947.3), p. 1.

and a vigorous sense of his own unique importance. With the spectacle before him of a kind of self-righteous Christian 'manager' on the one hand, and a series of bigoted secular 'messiahs' on the other, the modern thinker may well view Paul's self-understanding with some reserve. Nevertheless, Paul's view of vocation stands as a powerful expression of the potentialities of religious response, and can serve as a useful corrective to a secularized concept of Christian vocation.

The simplification and intensity of Paul's thinking about himself make inescapably evident that his self-understanding is one of responsiveness. As over against the modern enfeeblement of awareness of the divine, in Paul one sees a self completely absorbed in response to the holy. His 'prophetic' awareness of the holy is historical in the sense that it is mediated through a particular concrete event. It is also historical in the sense that the encounter makes Paul an active, participating worker in concrete activities in which the presence of the transcendent reality of Christ is mediated, so that concrete acts can be engaged in responsibly, yet they are also seen to be important for the fulfilment of God's transcendent purpose. Such an understanding can be an important corrective to the secularization of the meaning of vocation. To Paul there is only one calling, the service of Christ. The discovery that 'biblical' man is a 'whole man' has had great usefulness in theology, in breaking down false distinctions between the sacred and the secular. But if the 'whole man' is removed from the context of radical obedience, so that God is conceived as ministering to the whole man in his situation in this world, the result is destructive of any real awareness of the sacred. Paul knows himself to be laid hold of by Christ as a 'whole man', so that there is no aspect of his life, no energy, which is not to be brought into subjection to Christ. But he can have this confidence only after being cut off from the goals set by the conventions and power-structures of this world. Only if his activities are directed by the self-giving, open love which he meets in Christ can they be expressions of his vocation. Thus Paul offers a reminder that the frank acceptance of the self as important for God's work, which is a recurring feature of the prophetic-puritan tradition, bears within itself an important corrective to its tendency toward self-assertiveness.

It is of the essence of the prophetic-apostolic understanding of vocation that such a calling cannot be undertaken at one's own initiative, and it would be false to try to make it come alive again merely by an act of theological effort. Yet, as we have seen, an important note of Pauline vocation is his conviction that his task and calling are shared in a real measure by all the Church. Even though we cannot expect the Church in our time to see so direct a connexion as did Paul between its witness and the final fulfilment of the purpose of God, we may well strive to test our commitments and tasks by the measure of Paul's—that the true vocation of all is the calling to manifest in word and work the gospel and Spirit of Christ, and that patterns of work and achievement can have meaning in the context of faith only if in some significant way they can be vehicles for the expression of that Spirit of radical openness to the other. Such a test is a sobering one in our situation, in which so much of our effort is actually given to the maintenance of those social patterns and achievements which for Paul could be only a substructure of the real life and work of the believer. Yet it may be a salutary test, both as a reminder that it is false to try to discover ultimate meaning in all that we do—much of our activity must be written off as ultimately insignificant—and as a challenge to make our exploration of the theme of Christian vocation a thoroughgoing quest for honest and fruitful ways of living in the world but not by the standards of the world.

The suggestion that the ultimate test of work is its adequacy as a vehicle of the sensitive, self-forgetting love which the Christian encounters in Christ may seem to indicate that Christian vocation is ultimately socially irresponsible. Such a view may seem to imply that only immediately personal relations are relevant to decisions of love. Fully to deal with this question would lead beyond the scope of this study, but it can only be suggested here that in practice Christians who have envisaged their task as the ministering to a community of loving freedom have on the whole not been troubled so much by the temptation to irresponsibility ('antinomianism') as by the tendency to condense their version of love into legalism. Here again Paul can serve as a significant pathfinder, for he struggles in many ways with this very problem. Though he has often been considered a legalist, the whole thrust of his effort was against any legal solution of the ethical problem.[1] It is precisely his vision of the purpose of God beyond the immediate concerns of his work or his success which makes possible his restraint from legislating his own pattern. In his own sphere he stands as a significant example of 'detached commitment',[2] in which concrete goals are responsibly worked for, with full recognition that man does not find himself by achieving any of these goals, but only as his life and work find a place in God's ultimate order.

Finally, despite our honest hesitation to affirm that our own work has any significance in God's ultimate purpose, Paul's bold faith must confront our reticence here also. In any literalistic sense he was mistaken about his place in the divine purpose, yet his vision of man's work as significant for God remains valid for the Christian. Paul's faith that God had chosen to work through him may have meaning even in our situation in which the visible continuities of our history are only in the most fragmentary way, if at all, perceptibly related to God's ultimate purpose. As a man is drawn to a new understanding of himself by confronting the *agape* of God in Christ, he is cut off from the securities of position and power, and yet he is also drawn into responsible participation in a community which knows that it coheres through the spontaneous, generous love it meets in Christ. The task of expressing and implementing this love may be known in faith to be a task that God will in his own way take up and fulfil. A recent writer, pointing to the similarity of Jesus' message to that of Paul, writes perceptively,

> Thus the deeper meaning of Jesus' message is: in accepting one's death there is life for others; in suffering, there is glory; in submitting to judgement, one finds grace; in accepting one's finitude resides the only transcendence.[3]

Accepting this statement, we should only add—and here a study of Jesus would again reveal a parallel to Paul—that one who so accepts the negation of his own selfhood in the context of the love of God finds his deepest loyalty absorbed in a task of

[1] I Corinthians is as instructive as Romans on this point.
[2] For this phrase I am indebted to Professor J. Coert Rylaarsdam.
[3] James M. Robinson, *A New Quest of the Historical Jesus* (SBT 25), London, 1959, p. 123.

surpassing worth, the task of sharing the life of a community called to show God's own Spirit of love in its life. Though the enlistment of his energies in the service of this task may be imperfect, and though the visible results of his work may be temporary and fragmentary, he may know that 'in the Lord his labour is not in vain'.

II

MAN IN HISTORY

THE present study examines Paul's thought about man as a participant in history. So stated, it is apparent that Paul is approached with a modern question: In what ways can a man, or groups of men, participate significantly in the historical process? But though this question is a modern question, it is also an authentically Pauline question. Few ancient writings disclose the vigorous sense of vocation that appears in the letters of Paul. In many ways he makes evident his conviction that his individual life does have a place in 'history', though he would understand history (a word absent from his vocabulary) quite differently from most modern inquirers.

Though much modern interpretation of history despairs of finding meaning in history, when it does find meaning, this usually centres either on the concreteness of unique decision, in which the historical is the 'real' because it is the moment of responsibility and self-discovery, or on the involvement of the individual or group in a process leading towards a goal, in which the historical is 'real' because in it life is caught up into a process which leads to the fulfilment of its ultimate purpose. Paul was well aware, in his own terms, of these two poles around which so much thinking about history revolves. Indeed for him they were not separate foci, for it was through his own involvement in the supreme crisis of 'history' that he found himself as a free and responsible person.

THE STRUCTURE OF 'HISTORY'

A central theme in the Western interpretation of history has been the conviction that history moves toward a goal, and that somehow the goal gives meaning to what precedes. Since this conviction is largely a legacy of the Hebrew-Christian tradition, it is not surprising to find that Paul in his way shares it.[1] But the

[1] Cf. H. Cohen, quoted in K. Löwith, *Meaning in History*, Chicago, 1949, pp. 17 f.

'history' which moves toward a goal is very differently understood by Paul than it is by the usual modern thinker.[1]

If by 'history' is meant the total human experience in time, there is little reason for holding that history is for Paul an ordered process moving toward a goal. So far as the human experience as a whole has unity or order, it is the unity of mere continuity. E. F. Scott would go further and say that for Paul history in this sense evinces deterioration:

> Again, Paul has that historical sense which we sometimes think of as peculiar to the modern mind. He is aware that all events are mysteriously linked together, that the present must be understood in its relation to the great human drama which has been unfolding itself ever since time began. Paul's philosophy of history is indeed very different from ours. Instead of an unbroken progress from the lower to the higher he sees a continual deterioration.[2]

That aspect of Paul's thought which Scott formulates is most fully expressed in the first two chapters of Romans. Man's life may often find itself in the situation which Paul describes here, and if it is regarded simply as human experience, it shows mere continuity or deterioration. From Paul's point of view, however, more is involved than human experience. Even this sort of history is an encounter of God and man—an encounter of judgment. History in this sense is not an ordered process, but a resistance to God's order, and the results do not move toward a goal, but only to destruction. The fragmentary elements of good which exist in the life of men apart from Christ are unable to overcome the destructive forces, and cannot of themselves bring man's life to any goal. It would be possible to examine the theme of 'man

---

[1] For studies of the relation between biblical and modern interpretations of history, see K. Löwith, *op. cit.*; R. Niebuhr, *Faith and History*, London, 1949; H. Butterfield, *Christianity and History*, London, 1949; E. Vögelin, *Order and History*, vol. I *Israel and Revelation*, London, 1957; F. Sell, 'Geschichtserlebnis und Geschichtsanschauung', *Theologische Rundschau*, n.s. IX (1937), 94–135. For studies of Paul's view of history, see G. Schrenck, 'Die Geschichtsanschauung des Paulus auf dem Hintergrund seines Zeitalters', *Jahrbuch der theologischen Schule Bethel* III (1932), 59–86; H.-D. Wendland, *Geschichtsanschauung und Geschichtsbewusstsein im neuen Testament*, Göttingen, 1938; cf. also O. Cullmann, *Christ and Time* (ET), London, 1951; E. Stauffer, *New Testament Theology* (ET), London, 1955; R. Bultmann, *History and Eschatology*, Edinburgh, 1957, ch. 4.

[2] E. F. Scott, *Paul's Epistle to the Romans*, London, 1947, p. 107.

in history' in Paul's thought from this point of view, for from a purely quantitative point of view, most men have participated only in this history of judgment.[1]

However, the theme of judgment does not exhaust Paul's understanding of history, and in fact does not reach his most characteristic insight. For it is of the essence of his thought that human experience cannot be considered in itself; it does not, of itself, form a whole. God is the real actor in 'history'; there are events which compose an ordered whole and march toward a goal, but these are the acts of God, not of man. God is not contained in or exhausted by history, yet it is only his presence and action which constitute history; that is, which give order, cumulative meaning, and a goal to human activity and experience. The modern thinker may find it convenient to distinguish God's activity as a 'supra-historical factor',[2] but for Paul it would be better to define God's activity as the history-creating factor. 'History' is precisely the activity of God among men; it is God's act which redeems human life from mere continuity.

Since for Paul it is God's action which constitutes history, his view of history is 'mythological'. Jewish eschatological thought supplies the pattern through which he sees order in the course of time; in this pattern the tangible struggles of human communities are interwoven with the struggles of cosmic powers. 'This age'[3] is a sphere under the domination of trans-human spiritual forces. Paul can even speak of 'the god of this age'.[4] These unfriendly forces will ultimately be destroyed by Christ,[5] and already the power of Christ has effectively neutralized the hostile spiritual powers for those who have faith.[6] Viewed in the context of his own time, however, Paul puts little emphasis on angelic or demonic figures. Partly this results from his associating the

[1] The fruitfulness of the biblical insights into judgment in history, for the modern interpreter, is suggestively set forth by Butterfield, *op. cit.*, esp. ch. 3.

[2] C. H. Dodd, *The Bible Today*, Cambridge, 1946, p. 105.

[3] Rom. 12.2, etc.

[4] II Cor. 4.4. Here and in the previous reference the RSV translates as 'this world', but Paul's eschatological thought is better represented by the literal translation above. Cf. R. M. Grant, *Gnosticism and Early Christianity*, New York, 1959, p. 176.

[5] I Cor. 15.24.

[6] Rom. 8.35–39.

demonic forces with the natural creation rather than with history.[1] But this distinction is not rigidly observed. Though the cosmic powers are constitutive of the human situation, these sub-personal, compulsive factors do not create a history which moves towards a goal. The really 'historical' events are the encounters of God and man. Thus Satan is not mentioned in Paul's account of the Fall,[2] and though the demonic enslavement of man is recognized,[3] and 'sin' and 'law' are seen as compulsive forces which dominate man,[4] only God's acts give direction to man's life. God's work is seen in the past in the classic case of Abraham,[5] and (ambiguously) in Moses;[6] in the prophets, though these do not receive much attention by name from this point of view,[7] and definitively in Christ.[8] In Paul's own time, God's creative work continues in men like Paul himself.[9]

God is the maker of history, and where God is at work, human existence becomes more than mere continuity or self-destructiveness. While on the one hand, therefore, 'history' for Paul means man being drawn into a higher order of reality than can be perceived by the historian in the modern sense, on the other hand the powers of God's purpose are not wholly invisible in 'this world'. God has been at work in the history of the Hebrew and Jewish people.[10] This history, or rather, the activity of God which makes the story of this community a real history, is both real and visible. The story of the Hebrews, like its culmination in the story of Christ, can be 'openly set forth'.[11] The activity of God is a real event, and this is also true of God's activity in the Resurrection of Christ, which is the hinge on which the whole history swings from one age toward the other.[12] That God's action is real and visible does not mean that it will always be seen

[1] Stauffer, *NT Theology*, p. 64.
[2] Rom. 5.12–21.
[3] Gal. 4.3.
[4] Rom. 7.7–12.
[5] Rom. 4.11–12; Gal. 3.6–9.
[6] II Cor. 3.7.
[7] See below, ch. VI.
[8] Rom. 5.
[9] Rom. 15.18; I Cor. 15.10.
[10] Rom. 3.2; 9.4–5.
[11] Gal. 3.1 (RV).
[12] I Cor. 15.1–8.

as God's action. What is in fact the profoundest event of all may well appear to men as a 'stumbling block' or 'folly'.[1] God's action challenges men at precisely this point: what decision do you make about these events? The human response in faith (or the lack of it) is also part of the historical process.

The historical acts of God show themselves in visible acts of men. The history of the past is, in a sense, the history of God's undoing the work of 'Adam' or man. To Abraham a promise is made, and through Abraham this promise is passed on to later times. Moses and the Law represent a further step in God's action, though this is a step which for the moment even deepens the estrangement between God and man.[2] In Christ a decisive change in the human situation has taken place. And now in the present God still works in human acts, as Paul felt that he worked in himself.

The history which Paul regards as true history, then, is the activity which God has undertaken to counteract the essentially static situation of sin. This history is visible in real happenings, in a particular channel of human events—in a preliminary fashion in the Hebrew history and particularly in the story of Christ. Thus Paul sees real continuities in history, yet the mere concrete and temporally changing existence of the Hebrew-Jewish community does not constitute the history. For that is as much the history of rejection as it is the history of God's action.[3] The purpose of God all along has been to create a community, and for Paul this purpose has finally been achieved in the creation of the Church. The visible history of the Church is itself a concrete testimony to the work of God.[4] Yet in this case also there is much which is not the work of God, and the real nature of this visible group can be perceived only by faith.[5]

The history of God's action narrows down to its ultimate point in Christ. But this narrowness is only the prelude to the widest possible extension of community. God's action had

[1] I Cor. 1.23.
[2] Rom. 7.7–20.
[3] C. H. Dodd, *Romans* (MNTC), London, 1932, pp. 148–88. Even the failures of men may contribute to God's on-going purpose; cf. Rom. 11.11; I Cor. 10.11.
[4] I Thess. 1.6–10.
[5] I Cor. 1.10–25.

hitherto been confined to a narrow corridor, isolated from most of mankind by barriers which had become almost impassable. Now, all at once, not merely the successors to 'Moses', or even the descendants of 'Abraham', are made subject to God's working, but the whole race of Adam. For the first time, mankind as a whole can 'participate in history'. Thus while it is sometimes said that for Paul Christ is the end of history, and from one definition of history this is true, from the point of view of mankind at large entering into a meaningful process, Christ is the beginning of history: only now, and only in the period which Paul expects to be short, does mankind at large have an opportunity to be drawn into history at all.

Paul holds that God's action has created new possibilities of life in the present, and the newness of the 'now' is related to the visible history of Christ, and, behind him, of the Hebrew people. But history as Paul sees it stretches behind and beyond the present concrete history, which is set in a framework stretching from creation to consummation. The 'mythological' frame of reference is essential to Paul's thought, though he does not care to spin out the speculative details of past or future as did many apocalyptic writers. The framework is essential because it supplies, looking backward, an understanding of how the human situation came to be what it is, and of how God's action has met that situation. And, what interests Paul far more, looking beyond the present, the 'mythological' framework supplies an understanding of the goal toward which God's acts are moving. The consummation is already present, yet it is not wholly present.[1] The completion of God's promise requires that the powers of the new life, now at work in the Church through Christ, triumph completely. The formal structure of this hope is supplied largely by apocalyptic thought. Its personal content comes from the figure of Christ as known and remembered: 'Love never ends.'[2] To Paul it appeared that his gospel would be meaningless without a real future con-

---

[1] Most of the terms which Paul uses to describe the difference which Christ makes are used in both a present and a future reference; e.g., 'justification': *present*, Rom. 5.9; I Cor. 6.11; *future*, Rom. 2.13–16; 'adoption': *present*, Gal. 4.5–7; *future*, Rom. 8.23; 'life': *present*, Gal. 2.20; *future*, Rom. 6.8; 'glory': *present*, II Cor. 3.18; *future*, Rom. 5.2; 'salvation': *present*, I Cor. 1.18; *future*, Rom. 5.9.

[2] I Cor. 13.8.

summation, just as it would be meaningless without the real presence of new powers of life in Christ.[1]

Though the hope is an essential part of Paul's understanding of history, the 'now' is as frequently in the centre of his attention. 'Now' is a new kind of time, a time in which God's power, through Christ, is present and available to men in a new way.[2] The present time, filled with new possibilities, is from the point of view of the individual man characterized by the necessity for decision. Man in history is, as an individual, encountered by history and, so to speak, brought into history by the act of God in Christ and by his response to it. Man is not a primary actor, though he must respond. Whether or not he 'participates in history' is his decision. And the 'history' into which he is called is God's history, which God has shaped and which God will bring to fulfilment. Men, who have long been bound by a compulsion which they could not escape, may at last choose a new existence.

Thus from the point of view of faith and decision, the events of the past and even of the future sink into the background. God and man are brought together in Christ, and through Christ each man is faced with the necessity of deciding *now*.

But the self is not merely faced with existential decision. By faith he is incorporated into a new community. The contemporary history which concerns Paul is the history of the Church. Other 'historical' groupings, such as the Roman state, play a part in the divine plan, but only as a substructure of history, so to speak.[3] It is the Church that lives in expectation of the end, and even plays a part in God's chosen way of coming to the end. The individual thus has meaning in the historical process by virtue of the faith which unites him to the body of believers.[4] In the Church men participate in the life of Christ, become members of Christ, and find in Christ a Spirit which overcomes sin, and breaks down the various barriers which separate men. They find a new dimension of historical existence in that they find a new community. The Church lives paradoxically in two ages. It is the eschatological community of the last time, called into being by God. But

[1]I Cor. 15.
[2]Wendland (*Geschichtsanschauung*, p. 24) notes Paul's use of four different ways of describing the 'now'.
[3]Rom. 13.1–7.
[4]Wendland, *op. cit.*, p. 12.

it is not yet the ultimate community. It lives by hope—not the hope of gradual development, but the hope of a decisive future act of God which will terminate the existence of 'flesh' and 'sin'. Being such a group, its achievements do not have to be measured by their 'effects', for its life is 'hid with Christ in God'.[1] Its assurance of ultimate victory comes by faith.

On the other hand, the Church is a concrete sociological group. It contains people who have to get along together, who have to grow, who have to witness to their faith. And this side of its existence cannot be arbitrarily separated from the other. The man who is called into history by God through Christ finds himself in a community which has continuing temporal existence, and which must make an impact on the life of men through the use of means which are at least outwardly the same as means used by other communities. This type of historical existence is very different from what has been referred to above as the history of God's acts; yet it is not, in Paul's view, of an entirely different nature. The concrete growth of the Church, its increasing depth of appreciation of the riches of Christ, and also its increasing size and geographic spread, are parts of the total pattern of God's act. In the acts of the Church, in so far as they are really expressions of the Spirit of Christ, it is God who acts. All members of the Church thus take part in a forward-moving, concrete history, a history which expresses itself, though only partially, in the life and growth of a specific and visible organization. Paul leaves quite undecided the question of how extensive the 'growth' of the Church is to be. He does not think of the Church as encompassing and thus transforming the social institutions or practices of the society in which it lives, though he does insist on changes in the behaviour of individuals, to conform to the standards of the new society which they have entered; and in the society of the Church the new standards are intended to be effective. It is also the case that Paul thinks of the growth of the Church in terms of conflict and the overcoming of opposition, rather than in terms of the unfolding or developing of the new life to a gradually increasing climax. Yet here it must be remembered that conflict and even suffering are not for Paul purely passive states. Even suffering leads to victory, and though the victory to which it

[1]Col. 3.3.

leads is primarily in the future order, Paul's view of 'martyrdom' is characterized by a vigorous hope that suffering will produce results also in the present life of the Church.[1] On the whole, Paul pays little systematic attention to the question of growth. He was keenly aware of the persistence of the attitudes and powers of the 'old' life within the Church,[2] and of the opposition from without.[3] Yet when he thinks of God's purpose for human existence, he is filled with the keenest hope.[4] When he thinks of the churches or of his own work in and for the Church, from the point of view of God's purpose and God's presence, the same buoyant hope for an ultimate triumph of God appears in his attitude toward the empirical churches. God is at work in them; they will grow and triumph. One must say that Paul would have been very much surprised, had the Church grown numerically smaller. His whole expectation is that whatever impact the Church makes will be more, rather than less, with the passage of time.

None the less, Paul's confidence at this point poses peculiar difficulties for the modern interpreter, since what Paul recognized as 'the Church' does not closely correspond to what the modern interpreter finds the Church to be as he observes it. In part Paul's confidence in the progressive impact of the Christian proclamation could be maintained because he did not expect that the 'passage of time' would continue for long. The creation of the new people of God was a temporary task corresponding to a particular stage in the divine plan. Further, Paul held that entry into the Church involved a suspension of the standards and power structures of the surrounding secular society—a suspension which sprang not merely from a resolute act of will on the part of the community, but also from the presence in the Church of a world-destroying presence, the Spirit of Christ. He did not conceive the growth of the Church in terms of a growth in 'history' in the modern sense, in which the Church would be a factor in the interaction of the social forces of 'this world'.

The real 'outcome' of the life of the Church will not in any case

[1] See ch. VI.
[2] As in I Corinthians.
[3] As in I Thessalonians.
[4] Rom. 11.

be in its growth in this present order. The resurrection is the key to its history—for in the final resurrection the completion of God's purpose will be reached, and within that completion will be included the perfection of God's community and the final reward for each individual. For Paul, it is primarily the existence of the Church as a community which will find its fulfilment in the resurrection. The latter is not primarily a way of finding significance for the individual life, nor for the whole of history. A recent writer on the resurrection has commented as follows:

> That the *eschaton* of the Resurrection of Jesus, to which history is directed, does not mean a timeless transcendence, severed from all historical relations, is shown precisely by the Resurrected One, who is indeed the exalted, but none the less the historical Christ. Thereby history is not destroyed by the Resurrection, but resolved in a new reality.[1]

Künneth comments perceptively on the relation of the fulfilment of the future to the present; but for Paul the history which will be resolved in a new reality is the history of the Christian community. He has gone beyond a narrow particularism which saw God as concerned permanently with only one channel of human history. But he sees man's life as finding its fulfilment as it is incorporated into the Church. The channel is still narrow, though it is open to all, and spreading out into all the world.

Within the pattern of fulfilment, by which the life of every man may find new meaning in the present, and in the coming age a transformation into a new order of reality, there stands out in Paul's thought yet another mode of man's participation in history. By God's choice certain persons are given special tasks, which enlist all their energies, and in which their individual work is specially and consciously the channel for God's work. Paul expressed an amazingly vivid awareness of this sort of 'prophetic' vocation. So strong was his conviction that God was particularly at work within his work, that some scholars have believed that Paul thought his death to have a unique place in the eschatological pattern itself.[2] It appears that such a view overstates Paul's convictions about his personal role. Yet he believed that God worked

[1] W. Künneth, *Theologie der Auferstehung*, 4th ed., Munich, 1951, p. 219 (ET in preparation).
[2] See below, pp. 87–9.

in him, that his work was significant in the greatest crisis of God's purpose, and that, though he was only one among various 'apostles', he had a special and elevated role among them.

No sharp line can be drawn between the work of God in the Church, and the work of God in the chosen agent, the 'apostle'. Paul's understanding of himself represents a heightening of the awareness of God's presence which belongs to all who are 'in Christ'. Not merely the apostle, but each man, will be regarded individually by God, and the achievements of each will be taken up into the new order. Likewise Paul's conviction that his person and activity represent the person and activity of Christ is an intensification of a belief which applied more generally to the Church at large and to all its members. The specially chosen 'slave of Christ' or 'apostle' is marked, in the first place, by a keener consciousness of direct authorization and guidance by God, and, consequently, he is also distinguished by a more conscious knowledge of how he individually fits into God's work. He knows what he is doing, and sees at least in a measure how his work fits into the total pattern. It is also true that such especially chosen men were consequently men of leadership and authority in the Church. The element of authority in their understanding of themselves formed the most permanent legacy of the 'apostles' to the Church, but in Paul's own case this element was secondary.

Thus it is in the work of men specially chosen to participate in God's work that Paul brings together two important moments of understanding of history. For here history is an on-going process —not an empirical history of mankind, but a divine purpose actively and successively revealed, and in Paul's time reaching a decisive new level of partial fulfilment. And here too in vocation by Christ, the self is freed from its false existence, and takes part in work which contributes to the goal of God himself. In Paul's apostleship, his work is both wholehearted and conscious. He works with all his energies, yet all along he is aware that it is God who is working within him. History is continuous and purposive, yet not impersonal. It proceeds toward a goal, yet the goal is not distant and unrelated to the personal existence of the worker, for in the resurrection he will himself be taken up into the goal and become part of it.

PAUL AND MODERN POINTS OF VIEW

From this sketch of 'man in history' in Paul's thought, six different aspects of the participation of man in history may be abstracted. They are: man as the Man, Christ Jesus; man as sinner under judgment; man as unconscious and unwilling, yet contributing to God's purpose; man as historical in concrete, existential decision; man in the Church, finding a new place in history, by which his life participates in the true community and finds its consummation in a new future order; man as particularly chosen by God to carry out his work. These varying perspectives suggest points of contact with contemporary types of interpretation of history which may be noted briefly.

In the first place, the unique role of the Man, Christ Jesus falls largely outside the scope of this study. The meaning of Christ's manhood for Paul, and in particular its meaning for history, will be examined only to show that this meaning of manhood usually stands in sharp contrast to other ways in which man is significant in history, and, in particular, that it stands in contrast to the 'prophetic' conception of God's use of man that is characteristic of Paul himself. The only important parallel lies in the derivative similarity of 'imitation of Christ'.[1]

A second type of participation of man in history is that suggested by Paul's comments about the historical life of man at large. From this point of view history consists of mere continuity or deterioration. By faith the deterioration is seen to be judgment. Yet even this kind of history provides a necessary substratum for the special history of God's acts, and contains certain elements of good. There is a type of modern interpretation which would fix on this aspect of Paul's thought as 'Paul's view of history', and would perhaps also establish this view of history as normative for general interpretation of history.[2] Such views are representative of an aspect of Paul's thought and largely exhaust his understanding of the significance of most of what is now generally called 'history'. These interpretations do not fully do justice to Paul's thought, however, if they overlook the fact that Paul also held it to be God's purpose precisely to overcome the evil situation

[1]See ch. VII.
[2]Cf. Löwith, *Meaning in History*, *passim*.

36

which they describe so vividly, and that Paul held that God's power was actually at work in a community that was from one point of view a concrete social entity, the Church, to overcome the mere continuity of evil.

A third type of man's participation in history may be seen in Rom. 9–11. Here Paul describes God as working through unwilling agents. History here is purposive, moving toward a goal. But the men who live in history comprehend its purpose at best but dimly, and rebel against what they comprehend. Some modern interpretations of history make use of a Providence which works toward purposes of which the historical agents are unconscious. Such views may become so strongly teleological that the passing generations seem to have importance only through what they contribute to the final outcome. For Paul, the special mark of Israel's history is not that its participants were unconscious of God's purpose, but that they rebelled against it, and yet in spite of their rebellion they served God's purpose. In fact, the sin of Israel has actually hastened the accomplishment of God's aim.[1] From Paul's point of view, the insight into the way in which God can make use of even unwilling agents is a minor one. It is, of course, a restatement of an old prophetic theme.[2] The conviction that history has a direction and purpose, combined with the recognition that men often ignore and rebel against that purpose, has proved fruitful for contemporary thinkers of various schools.[3] From the point of view of an adequate representation of Paul's thought, this insight represents an important way of understanding the past and of illuminating one difficult problem (the role of Israel in the divine plan), rather than a principal ingredient of 'history' which occupied most of his attention.

A fourth type of relation of man to history is seen in the Pauline conception of faith and decision. Here past and future recede from the centre of attention and all is concentrated on 'the moment'.[4] This 'existentialist' phase of history does not look

[1] Rom. 11.11.
[2] Cf. Isa. 42.19, and the many quotations, mostly from Isaiah, used by Paul in Rom. 9–11.
[3] Cf. esp. Butterfield, *op. cit.*, ch. 5.
[4] Faith has a very different meaning in the Letter to the Hebrews, and is there related to history in a very different way; cf. Heb. 11. The plan and dynamic of history come from God; indeed the poignancy of ch. 11 comes

at the temporal framework, but at present decision. Human life finds actuality in decision, and the real decision is the one by which man is confronted in Christ. A profound point of contact exists between Paul and the contemporary existentialist. But as an interpretation of Paul's thought, a pure existentialism is weak at two points: it tends to emphasize human decision rather than divine action, and it under-values Paul's convictions about the continuity and purpose of man's life under God. For the existentialist, it is man's 'decision', not his 'work', that counts. For Paul it is both.[1]

A fifth type of participation of man in history is seen in the life of the Church. Here man's historical life consists both of faith 'moment by moment', and of work which is God's work leading toward God's goal. For Paul the antinomy between the finding of meaning in contemporary, actual existence, and the finding of meaning in the ultimate goal, is resolved by a faith that men's lives in Christ receive both kinds of meaning.

Movement of history toward a goal has been a prominent feature of both liberal-progressive and '*heilsgeschichtlich*' interpretations of history. Real points of contact between Paul's thought

---

from the fact that even the wonderful faith of the Old Testament heroes could not bring them to that reality which God has brought to men in Christ. (Cf. Heb. 12.1–2.) Yet, in a limited sense, faith creates history. Those who see the unseen and have here no abiding city are the ones through whom the unseen becomes actualized. Cf. O. Michel, *Der Brief an die Hebräer* (Krit.-Exeg. Comm. über N.T.), 9th ed., Göttingen, 1955, pp. 247–9; R. N. Flew, *The Idea of Perfection in Christian Theology*, London, 1934, ch. 3; Heinrich Barth, 'Christliche und idealistische Deutung der Geschichte', *Zwischen den Zeiten* III (1925), 154–82.

Something analogous to the thought of Hebrews appears in Paul, for whom the faith of Abraham is a critical element in the history of the past, and for whom men may still achieve real results in history only by participation in the powers of the new age. But Paul never works out the idea that faith in the future creates history for several reasons: (1) when he thinks of the long stream of history, it is God's purpose, not the human struggle, that he sees, in contrast to Heb. 11; (2) consequently, man's historical role is seen vividly only in relation to the present; (3) in the present, man's power to participate in history comes not so much from his grasp of something yet to come ('hope' in Paul's vocabulary, rather than 'faith'), as from the Christ who has come in the past and lives in the present.

[1] Cf. esp. R. Bultmann, 'Heilsgeschichte und Geschichte', *Theologische Literaturzeitung* LXXIII (1948), cols. 659–66; *History and Eschatology*, esp. chs. 8 and 9; 'History of Salvation and History', *Existence and Faith*, New York, 1960, pp. 226–40, etc.

and that of the liberal progressive view are slight. Yet it would be incorrect to deny them altogether. The basis for such a contact is Paul's confidence that the power of Christ was really at work in the present life. Hence he could be hopeful about his own work and influence, and about the growth of the churches. These facts have made it possible for liberal-progressive interpreters of history to find a point of contact with Paul, though a progressive view of history could scarcely be developed from Paul as a base.[1] The great difference is that for Paul, cumulative results in this world, while not impossible, are more or less incidental. He insists that such results can be real only as they derive from Christ, but as men come to faith in Christ they are not brought to a life of in-action, defeatism, or failure. History is genuinely 'progressive', in that it moves toward a grand consummation. Though this consummation will never be reached by means of human achieve-ments in this order, or even by means of God's work through man in this world, nevertheless results in this order are not excluded. Paul fully expects that they will appear. He differs from modern progressive views of history in his conviction that the goal will not be reached by cumulative achievements in this world, in his concentration on a small area of the total of human experi-ence as the genuine 'history', in his firm insistence that it is God, not man, who is the maker of history, and in his conviction that such 'results' as may be achieved within the Church are not to be derived from immanent, this-worldly powers.

The '*heilsgeschichtlich*' interpreters of history offer, on the whole, the most adequate representation of Paul's understanding of the overall pattern of history, even though many who interpret the New Testament from this point of view do not fully sense the difficulty of making this perspective relevant in the context of contemporary Christian faith. They see history as directed by God's will, and composed of his acts. They recognize that God is seriously 'involved in time'. They see that God's purpose draws men into history.[2] For such interpreters the problematical point is always this also very critical one: What is the nature of the present time, in which both old and new ages in some sense

[1] Cf. W. Rauschenbusch, *Christianity and the Social Crisis*, New York, 1907, pp. 102–5, who finds little support in Paul.
[2] Cf. esp. Cullmann, *Christ and Time*; Stauffer, *NT Theology*.

run concurrently ? Paul was full of faith that in spite of the terrible power of evil, for those who had faith, life in a new dimension was real through Christ. The distinction was black-and-white: within only one visible and known community was the new power at work. In what sense this confidence of Paul can be asserted about the Church of today is one of the most difficult of theological problems.[1]

Finally, a sixth type of participation of man in history is that to which this study is principally devoted—the work of God through his specially chosen and individually responsible apostle or slave. Here his immense confidence of God's presence lends dignity, authority, and tremendous vitality to the worker, who believes that he himself 'creates history', not only in this present time but for the coming age. And here the agent of God is consciously aware of the part which he plays in God's economy.

For the modern interpreter of history this view, so clearly evident in Paul, presents great difficulties. Modern man must perforce be concerned with a much wider range of 'history' than was Paul—a wide range of contemporary life. This makes it difficult to achieve the single-minded confidence of Paul, that he could know what sort of fruit his work would bear. Even more difficult for the modern Christian is the bold and free faith of Paul that what he did, Christ did—so that he almost never felt called upon to apologize. Few in modern times have dared so vigorously to assert their faith in divine guidance and divine presence. The early Friends provide perhaps the nearest analogy.[2] Clearly the modern 'imitator' of Paul could easily become a bigoted 'Messiah', just as many have felt that Paul himself was such a bigot. Secular versions of such convictions are well known today. They show a dynamic often similar to that of Paul, but lack the controls which he found in Christ.

Recognizing these difficulties, we have indicated in the previous chapter some of the ways in which Paul's understanding of his call 'into history' is still significant. We turn now to study it in detail.

[1]Cf. T. Preiss, 'The vision of history in the New Testament' in *Life in Christ* (ET) (SBT 13), London, 1954, pp. 61–80.
[2]Cf. George Fox, *Journal* (Everyman's Library), London, 1944.

III

WORK AND ITS RESULTS

P<small>AUL</small>'s understanding of man's achievement is well expressed in what he says about work. At first sight the function of work may seem remote from the sphere of history and eschatology. But Paul places work in an eschatological setting, seeing it as a response to God's call and command, in relation to God's purpose. He finds that not only the great 'work' of proclaiming the gospel, but also the daily round of labour by any believer, participates in a new order already being created by God through Christ.[1]

For Paul, the significance of man's work springs from its relation to the new community, the Church. Work in relation to the 'old' order, the society external to the Church, interests him but slightly. Such work indeed provides a kind of environment for the existence of God's new creation, the Church. And many of the forms of work performed in society at large are also performed in the new community—where, however, they take on an entirely new significance. But the structures of the 'old' society in which work takes place are not important. In this sense it is hardly too much to say that the Church is a community free from all historical relationships.[2] Yet the Church takes up into itself the strivings which had manifested themselves in the structures of pagan and Jewish society, and thus becomes a fulfilment of them. In the Church, God has created a situation in which men can truly work, and work with enduring results.

The meaning of work for Paul will be presented by studying first work apart from Christ, then the work of proclaiming the gospel, and finally work in its ordinary sense as performed within the context of the Church.

---

[1] On work in Paul see especially G. Bertram, *'ergon'*, *TWNT*, II, 631–53; F. Hauck, *'Kopos, kopiaō'*, *TWNT*, III, 827–9; W. Bienert, *Die Arbeit nach der Lehre der Bibel*, 2nd ed., Stuttgart, 1956, chs. 3 and 4; Alan Richardson, *The Biblical Doctrine of Work*, London, 1952.

[2] E. Lohmeyer, *Grundlagen paulinischer Theologie*, Tübingen, 1929, p. 205.

WORK APART FROM CHRIST

The activities of men apart from Christ are seldom called 'work' by Paul, except in connexion with the problem of faith and works. Indeed, a major theme of Paul's thought about the life of man apart from Christ is the utter futility and lack of achievement of such a life.[1] Such lives are twisted and empty. The mind becomes useless or counterfeit, and the resulting activities tend to be guided by desire or passion.[2] Paul recognizes a controlling factor, the conscience, but it is thought of as a factor which evaluates action after it has taken place, not as a guiding principle.[3] Men are caught in the compulsive power of an almost demonic force, 'sin', which overcomes and perverts whatever efforts they make toward obedience.[4] The result of such lives could only be 'evil works',[5] the 'works of darkness' which the apostle urges his readers to cast off,[6] the 'works of the flesh' of which he gives a vivid list.[7] A phrase from Ephesians summarizes the two aspects of Paul's thought: 'Take no part in the unfruitful works of darkness.'[8] The works of men apart from Christ belong to the sphere of 'darkness', and they are consequently 'unfruitful'; they do not produce any results which God will allow to continue as permanent or real.

This picture of the human situation is not basically altered by the presence of the law. The law makes clearer to men their inner striving to work at something. It lays down for them the kind of activity that is good and meets God's approval, although apart from the law men already had some inkling of the divine demands.[9] Paul discusses the 'works of the law' in Romans and Galatians; elsewhere the term 'works' is not used in this connexion.[10] His views here are well known. The law is good. It shows the kind

[1]Rom. 1.18–3.20.
[2]Rom. 1.21–28.
[3]Rom. 2.15. See C. A. Pierce, *Conscience in the New Testament* (SBT 15), London, 1955, esp. ch. 9.
[4]Rom. 5.12–14; 7.7–21.
[5]Col. 1.21.
[6]Rom. 13.12.
[7]Gal. 5.19–21.
[8]Eph. 5.11.
[9]Rom. 3.19; 2.15.
[10]But cf. Eph. 2.9.

of thing God really wants men to do; in a word, the total of all its requirements is love.[1] But the law only intensified the human problem, partly by the increasing awareness of sin which it made inevitable,[2] and also because the presence of this clear pattern only intensified the effort of the self to justify itself, to make itself good enough to encounter God.[3] The striving to find a position in which one can encounter God gives the nuance to Paul's phrase, 'works of the law', and his attention is not fixed on the specific activities but on this deeper end, which, he holds, they are performed to achieve. Hence, in spite of very real achievements at specific points, in its net result the law has not changed the pattern of human life. Men strive to do something that will achieve real results; they try to 'work'. But even when the law 'came in' as a guiding principle, and directed men to an activity that was real work, aimed at achieving God's purposes, this law with its works was unable to produce any real results. In spite of his works the man who lived under the law was not better than others, both because the works of the law were not rigorously and sincerely carried out,[4] and even more profoundly because they could not be, since the law could not overcome the force of sin, which took hold of men's 'flesh' and frustrated the attempt to give allegiance to the commandments of God.[5] Hence the works of the law remain in the domain of the flesh, and the law itself is linked to the flesh. Even this attempt at obedience testifies to the painful solidarity of men in failure to obey God.[6]

None the less, the failure of pagans and Jews does not mean that life apart from Christ has nothing in common with the new creation inaugurated by Christ. 'Work' in the sense of working for a living is one of the areas common to men inside and beyond the community of faith; that the two groups have something in common is made clear by Paul's advice to work in order to make a good impression on outsiders.[7] Such common ground is also pre-

[1]Rom. 13.9-10.
[2]Rom. 3.20; 7.7-14.
[3]Rom. 3.9-20; Gal. 3.10-14.
[4]Rom. 2.1-3.
[5]Rom. 7.
[6]See Bo Reicke, 'The law and this world according to Paul', *JBL* LXX (1951), 259-76.
[7]I Thess. 4.11-12.

supposed in the assumption that there is a moral order in the sphere of work: 'If any man will not work, neither let him eat.'[1] Similarly Paul maintains that the work of maintaining political order is divinely ordained.[2] Political power, with its purpose of exercising retributive justice, performs a valid kind of work within its limits, even though it acts in precisely the way in which Christians do not act, for they do not exact retribution.[3]

Thus Paul's evaluation of men's work apart from Christ is similar to his judgment on human life in general. From within the Christian community a point of contact can be seen with the obligation and striving to labour which are found in the old order of society, just as from outside the community men may recognize something of the Christians' spirit by their devotion to their task. The passing comments on work thus reveal a typical pattern of Pauline thought—life apart from Christ does not receive attention as a thing in itself, yet Paul recognizes in the world a kind of substratum for the full life of the community of Christ, which forms a basis for later thinking about the problem of natural theology.

These fragments of meaning in the world spring from God's creative purpose, and result in certain partial achievements. Yet the recognition of elements of goodness in the world, and of fragmentary achievements, does not fundamentally affect Paul's conviction that all work apart from Christ is ultimately futile because it does not 'come out' anywhere. It does not fit into a larger whole which guarantees its completion and fulfilment. On the contrary, whatever elements there are of good are contradicted and ultimately destroyed by the violent forces of evil at work in man and in the world. Unlike some who stand in the Judeo-Christian apocalyptic tradition, however, Paul shows little interest

---

[1]II Thess. 3.10; cf. vv. 6–15. No exact parallel to this saying is known; the nearest are found in the sayings of Jewish rabbis. The rabbis, following the tradition of Jewish wisdom, present the demand to work as a 'natural' necessity. ('If a man will not work, he shall not eat.') Paul presents a 'moral' necessity to the community to deprive the idle of charitable help. But these emphases are not so different as Bienert, *Die Arbeit*, p. 368, maintains. The transfer of common sense insights into moral teaching often involved a similar recognition that the results must be enforced, and do not necessarily flow automatically from good and bad action.

[2]Rom. 13.1–7.

[3]Rom. 12.19–21; cf. O. Cullmann, *The State in the New Testament*, London, 1957, ch. 3.

in articulating these destructive forces into a 'history of evil'. His thought is too firmly fixed on God and man for him to dwell on this speculative subject.

Thus human work is subject to judgment. Man is judged by his 'work'; that is, his life is tested by its results.[1] The ultimate end of the world is a subject on which Paul does not dwell in detail, but his common judgment on human activities is that apart from Christ, 'the end of those things is death'.[2] They have no outcome or permanent results. In the face of this conviction of the utter futility of men's striving to achieve something permanent and good, the question of eternal punishment sinks into the background and is never really discussed. To say that God brings men and their works to nothing is sufficient judgment.[3]

PAUL'S WORK OF PROCLAMATION

For Paul, the coming of Christ inaugurated a new era in which men may be delivered from this blind alley. By faith men are enabled to come into God's presence. By virtue of their identification with Christ, God counts them just;[4] and a new eschatological power, the presence of Christ or the Spirit, enables them at last to live, and to accomplish that which in their frustrated way they had tried to do before.[5]

Thus though 'works' are pushed aside, that does not mean that 'work' is. In fact, most of what Paul has to say about man's work does not deal with the activities of men apart from Christ, or with the works of the law, but with the kind of work which appears to him to be the only real work of man: the work which is performed by the followers of Christ. This is at once man's work, in which he for the first time becomes really wholehearted in his devotion to a task,[6] and in which he for the first time really

[1]Rom. 2.6, etc.
[2]Rom. 6.21.
[3]In II Thess. 1.9, Paul speaks of 'eternal destruction from the face of the Lord'. Whether with F. V. Filson (*St Paul's Conception of Recompense*, Leipzig, 1931, p. 76) it is held that 'death' implies eternal punishment, or whether with Millar Burrows (*An Outline of Biblical Theology*, Philadelphia, 1946, p. 211) 'death' is perhaps to be taken literally, the important point is that Paul does not clearly state his understanding of this speculative point.
[4]Rom. 3.21–30.
[5]Gal. 2.20–21; cf. Rom. 7–8.
[6]Col. 1.29.

accomplishes something;[1] it is also God's work, or Christ's, for the energy that activates the worker is the very presence of God's or Christ's spirit.[2] While for Paul *the* work is the work of creating the new Church of Christ, all one's labour—even that of the most insignificant member of the church—is drawn into the new sphere in which labour is not in vain.[3] These affirmations must now be examined in greater detail.

Paul's view of his own work provides the clearest statement of his understanding of man's work 'in Christ' or in the Church. Yet Paul does not think of himself as unique. He speaks frequently of his 'fellow-workers', and those who are mentioned as fellow-workers include a wide range of associates.[4] No fixed list or rank is designated by the term; it indicates the sharing of a common task. Likewise, when he speaks of God's work, he does not confine it to a special group, but points sometimes to the activity of God in and through himself,[5] and sometimes to God's work in the community.[6]

It is within the Church that Paul sees work achieving real results. In fact, the real 'work' for him is the proclaiming of the gospel and the upbuilding of the Christian Church. Other activities, including those of unbelievers, can only contribute indirectly to this end, or provide the prerequisite conditions. Within the new eschatological community, the Church, there is no distinction between 'sacred' and 'secular' activities, so long as they are devoted to the end of building up the community. Hence all work takes on new meaning, and contributes to the realizing of ends both in this age and in the age to come. Paul's own work provides the model for his understanding of work, and most of the following discussion will be drawn from what he says about his own work.

A first characteristic of the work within and for the community of Christ is its wholeheartedness. It is marked by complete and

[1] I Cor. 15.10, 58.
[2] I Cor. 2.4–5.
[3] I Cor. 15.58.
[4] *Synergos*, used twelve times in singular and plural; the term was well-established in *Koinē* Greek, but appears in the Greek Bible only in II Macc. 8.7; 14.5, and III John 8 outside of Paul's letters. Those mentioned as fellow-workers include Prisca and Aquila, Urbanus, and Timothy (Rom. 16.3, 9, 21); and others (Phil. 4.3; Col. 4.11; Philemon 1, 24).
[5] I Cor. 15.10.
[6] Rom. 14.20; Phil. 1.6.

self-forgetting devotion to the task. Whatever the relation of Romans, chapters 7 and 8, to Paul's own biography, it is clear that the contrast between frustrated tension in chapter 7 and complete devotion in chapter 8 is the contrast between man's life and activity apart from and with the Spirit of Christ.[1]

It is largely in the light of this aspect of work—its demand for all the resources of one's life—that Paul's fondness for the term 'labour' is to be understood.[2] This noun and verb, in ordinary Greek usage, indicated work as fatiguing, or fatigue itself. In Paul they include this meaning, and may mean simply 'trouble'.[3] But the common reference of the term 'labour' in Paul is very different. 'Labour' suggests something that a man does vigorously, putting all that he has into it, and getting results. In his usage it thus acquires a decidedly active meaning. Passive suffering he is aware of, and discusses using other terms.[4] He sees suffering in an eschatological orientation; 'For this slight momentary affliction is preparing for us an eternal weight of glory beyond all comparison.'[5] No man can choose for himself whether or not such afflictions are to be his lot, though Paul expects them to be the normal lot of the Christian. Yet on the whole it is fair to say that the whole 'problem of suffering', which plays such a large part in many sections of the Old Testament, is no longer central for Paul. His mind is on other things.[6] Thus an eschatological orientation toward labour in the sense of 'painful duty now; then, reward', would be a very incomplete expression of Paul's thought.[7]

[1]Rom. 7.15–25; 8.31–9. Cf. W. G. Kümmel, *Das Bild des Menschen im Neuen Testament*, Zurich, 1948, pp. 32 f.; C. H. Dodd, *Romans* (MNTC), London, 1932, pp. 107 f.

[2]*Kopos*. See F. Hauck, *TWNT*, III, 827–9; Beinert, *Die Arbeit*, p. 316. The term also has a connexion with Paul's use of the metaphor of slavery, since it was used of the slave's labour.

[3]He associates *kopos* (labour) three times with *mochthos* ('toil') a term even more indicative of exhaustion.

[4]The commonest term to express this is *thlipsis* ('affliction' or 'trouble').

[5]II Cor. 4.17; cf. Rom. 8.18, and the encouragement given to the Thessalonians: I Thess. 2.14–16.

[6]'He is so absorbed in his "Gospel" that [his stormy background] makes very little impression on him.' Sanday and Headlam, p. 125 (on Rom. 5.3). See below, pp. 111–15.

[7]*Kopos* is used in this way in Rev. 15.13: '. . . that they may rest from their labours.' This usage has its background in the LXX, where the term refers to the troubles of the righteous. Cf. Ps. 25(24).18; Isa. 65.23; and Hauck, *TWNT*, III, 828.

He does not use the metaphor of 'rest' for the reward to come in the future. For Paul, 'labour' suggests exhausting labour, but the things which interest him are not the painfulness and fatigue of the work, but the engrossment in the task on the one hand, and the achieving of results on the other.[1] The startling list of hardships which he feels driven to enumerate to the Corinthians serves to demonstrate how completely he has devoted himself as a servant of Christ.[2] He refers in the same way to his labours in the less controversial Thessalonian letters, where the reference is more specifically to his earning a living in order to be free to please God and not men.[3] In another passage he lists a formidable series of hardships and labours, engaged in to 'put no obstacle in any one's way'.[4] In all of these cases the term 'labour' suggests strenuous work, and also implies the complete devotion which he had found impossible in any other setting for work.

Even more characteristic of Paul was his keen conviction that work 'in Christ' will bear fruit—that it is not mere activity, but real work which will produce something. It was part of the common-sense wisdom of the ancient world that work was more than mere activity; it is directed to a useful end.[5] But the faith that man's various works might not merely be useful and endure, but even be a meaningful part of a cumulative divine purpose, was particularly the mark of the Hebrew-Jewish tradition. Thus Jeremiah, for instance, understood his prophetic vocation.[6] In later Judaism the hope of the resurrection enabled Jews to believe that they would themselves participate in the new order which God would create and to which, in some small measure, their labours might contribute.[7] Thus a faith which was basically

[1]The warnings of Paul against fatigue, and his awareness of his own fatigue, are noted by Ethelbert Stauffer, who links these themes with the idea of fatigue and laboriousness as an aspect of punishment for sin (cf. Gen. 3.17-19). But this is not the note which dominates Paul's comments on labour. Cf. Stauffer, *NT Theology*, p. 71. 'Rest' is in II Thess. 1.7 only.

[2]II Cor. 11.23-28. Here 'labours' head the list of the marks of the true servant of Christ.

[3]I Thess. 2.9.

[4]II Cor. 6.3-7; cf. II Thess. 3.8-9.

[5]Cf. e.g., Hesiod, *Works and Days*, 307 ff., cited in Bertram, *TWNT*, II, 632.

[6]Jer. 1.4-10, 17-19.

[7]Dan. 12.1-3. Cf. J. Bonsirven, *Le Judaïsme palestinien au temps de Jésus-Christ*, 2nd ed., Paris, 1934-5, I, p. 468.

oriented towards vindicating the reality of God's righteousness served also to vindicate the reality of human achievement. Negatively, the corrosive effects of doubt about the reality of final achievement can be seen in Koheleth.[1] The faith of the prophets, that a man could be called by God to work in his work, appears for the community of faith in the vivid sense of a special eschatological vocation shown in the writings of Qumran.[2]

Paul continues the typically Hebraic concern that a man's activity be in such relation to God that it may have permanent, cumulative result. His hope is grounded in a conception of God at work in the present, making real a new kind of community, into which men are called and in which their efforts bear real results. He makes no rigid disjunction between results in the here and now, and results in the world to come.

It is Paul's confident expectation that as long as he lives 'in the flesh' it will be possible for him to work, and to work with results. He thinks in the first place of visible, 'this-worldly' results, in terms of building up Christian churches.[3] When he plans a visit to Rome, he intends it to have results.[4] In his struggle to maintain his position at Corinth, he frequently cited the results as evidence of the genuineness of his work as a representative of Christ. The Corinthian community itself is his production.[5] He is their 'father'.[6] He has laboured 'more abundantly' than the other apostles; the context shows clearly that the excess includes the greater result as well as the greater activity.[7]

The communities which he founded, Paul expected, would endure to the end—which was probably near.[8] Not only so, but the results are to be cumulative, for he hopes that his work will

---

[1] Eccles. 1.9–11; 2.18–23.
[2] See, for instance, 'The War of the Sons of Light and the Sons of Darkness', *passim*, in Theodor H. Gaster, *The Scriptures of the Dead Sea Sect*, London, 1957, pp. 261–84.
[3] Phil. 1.22: 'fruitful labour'.
[4] Rom. 1.13: 'that I may reap some harvest among you.'
[5] I Cor. 9.1: 'Are not you my workmanship in the Lord?' Cf. I Cor. 1.6: 'So your experience has confirmed the testimony that I bore to Christ' (Goodspeed's trans.). Cf. James Moffatt, *I Corinthians* (MNTC), London, 1938, p. 7.
[6] I Cor. 4.14–15.
[7] I Cor. 15.10. Cf. A. Robertson and A. Plummer, *I Corinthians* (ICC), Edinburgh, 1911, p. 342.
[8] I Thess. 4.13–18; Rom. 13.11.

be continued by others. 'I do hope that as your faith increases, my influence may be immensely enlarged through you.'[1] It has often been observed that a confidence in the cumulative results of his work lay behind Paul's bold plan of preaching the gospel to the whole Gentile world, and dictated his procedure of starting in strategic centres from which new work would spring.[2] It is true that Paul was not a modern man and may well have thought of the 'whole world' representatively; that is, each group, rather than each individual, must be reached.[3] Such may have been Paul's interpretation of the tradition represented by Mark 13.10: 'And the gospel must first be preached to all nations.' But if so, his eschatological theory was joined to a vivid sense of the necessity of reaching as many as possible, as is shown by his enlistment of co-workers and his concern for the growth of his churches.[4]

Paul recognized contingency in results of this kind. The Church in one sense lives by the powers of the new age; in another, it is still in the old era in which the opposition to God can triumph. Some very real achievements may take place, which he hopes will endure. But in any concrete case the work may come to nothing. Paul's doubts about the endurance of his work do not, however, flow from any doubts about the validity of his own contribution. He seldom expresses regret for anything that he has done. The contingency depends on other factors in the situation, and particularly on the work of those who try to undo his work. The 'open' character of the historical outcome is apparent in the struggles in the Galatian and Corinthian churches. Here were cases of conflict, in which the result was not determined until the conflict was over.

However, in spite of the doubtfulness of each specific instance, the dominant note of Paul's thought is one of achievement and success. There may, even will, be failures in concrete cases, but on the whole the work goes forward; indeed it must, since God is active in it.

A favourite term in which the tangible results may be expressed

[1]II Cor. 10.15 (Goodspeed's trans.).
[2]Rom. 15.17-21; E. F. Scott, *Paul's Epistle to the Romans*, p. 18.
[3]Johannes Munck, *Paul and the Salvation of Mankind* (ET), London, 1959, pp. 48-55.
[4]Cf. I Cor. 9.15-23.

is *karpos*, fruit.[1] Sometimes the term refers to the changes in character produced in the Christian life generally.[2] Negatively, it may point to the unfruitfulness of life apart from Christ.[3] In Rom. 6.22, the 'fruit' or immediate result of being a servant of God is 'sanctification';[4] the 'end' or final result is eternal life. The contrast is typical of *karpos*, which consistently refers to results in this order. Again, the term is used of the contribution which the Gentile churches were to send to Jerusalem; the offering must actually be delivered before it is really a fruitful act.[5] Similarly, it refers to the credit which the Philippians have gained through their gift to Paul.[6] In other cases, it describes the visible results of Paul's own activities.[7]

Paul's pre-occupation with success appears strongly in his concern lest he work 'in vain'. He comments that his visit to Thessalonica was 'no failure'.[8] The struggle with the threat of failure is a constant one with him.[9] The contact with a similar theme in the Old Testament is worth noting.[10] His interest in results appears in the meaning which he gives to the term 'senseless', which becomes an equivalent of 'in vain'.[11]

---

[1]So also commonly in the *Koinē*. Cf. F. Hauck, '*karpos*', *TWNT*, III, 617–18.

[2]Rom. 6.22; Gal. 5.22; Phil. 1.11; cf. Eph. 5.9.

[3]Rom. 6.21; cf. *akarpos*, Eph. 5.11; this term is used with a different reference in I Cor. 14.14.

[4]Literally 'the process of becoming fitted for the service of God'. Cf. Sanday and Headlam, p. 169. For Paul, the term implies moral transformation of character; cf. I Thess. 4.3–7.

[5]Rom. 15.28.

[6]Phil. 4.17.

[7]Rom. 1.13; Phil. 1.22.

[8]I Thess. 2.1 (Moffatt's trans.).

[9]Cf. I Cor. 15.10, 58; II Cor. 6.1; Gal. 2.2; Phil. 2.16; I Thess. 3.5. *Kenos* with the meaning 'without *result*' appears in Paul eight times; with the meaning 'without *content*' only four times including once in Ephesians. Cf. W. F. Arndt and F. W. Gingrich, *A Greek-English Lexicon of the New Testament*, Cambridge and Chicago, 1957, *s.v.*

[10]'. . . So that in the day of Christ I may be proud that I did not run in vain or labour in vain' (Phil. 2.16), is a reflection of Isa. 49.4; 65.23.

[11]Cf. Gal. 4.11 with the passages cited in n. 9 above. Commonly *eikē* means 'senseless', 'without reason', or 'without purpose'. Paul uses this word five times, of which two must bear the meaning 'without *result*' (Gal. 3.4; 4.11), while two others may include this meaning (I Cor. 15.2; Rom. 13.4). In Col. 2.18, *eikē* means 'without reason'. Liddell and Scott, *s.v.*, cite an instance of the meaning 'without result' from the papyri; Arndt and Gingrich,

The 'fruit' or result of Paul's work, or, correspondingly, the result of the activity of the Spirit of God, is thus sometimes described concretely in terms of the building up of communities, and in terms of specific acts of these communities, e.g., gifts of money. Behind these stand the less concrete but equally real results in terms of the transformation of personalities. Here is a reminder that for Paul what happened was not simply the building up of an organization, but the introduction of a new kind of life. When he thought of the continuance or cumulative effect of the labour of the community of Christ, it was primarily with this transformation that he was concerned. The organization is necessary, and its leaders are to be respected. In a special sense they are workers for God.[1] He is particularly sensitive about his own position of authority.[2] But the organization as such, and its officials, do not assume the importance in Paul's own letters that they later acquire.[3]

The 'fruit' of Paul's work, or that of other leaders and of churches, produces none the less changes in the visible course of events. Paul hopes that these changes will continue in effect and will, through the work of others, be of increasing effect. This hope, and the extent of its significance for Paul's thought, will be discussed below, in connexion with the subject of 'growth'.[4]

It is because the 'real events' in this age were not primarily tangible events of an organizational sort, but inward transformations, that Paul can so closely relate the 'results'[5] in this age with the 'reward'[6] in the age to come. Along with Paul's insistence that man is saved and rendered acceptable to God by faith only,

---

s.v., cite one instance of this meaning outside of Paul (Lucian, *Anacharsis* 19). Both of these lexicons cite more frequent attestation for other meanings. *TWNT*, Preisigke, and Moulton and Milligan do not cite any reference to the meaning 'without result'. Thus it appears that while Paul was not coining a special usage, his interest in results gave his use of the term *eikē* a special flavour. Cf., *s.v.*, *TWNT*; F. Preisigke, *Wörterbuch der griechischen Papyrusurkunden*, ed. E. Kiessling, Berlin, 1925–31; J. H. Moulton and G. Milligan, *The Vocabulary of the Greek New Testament*, London, 1930.

[1] I Thess. 5.12.
[2] I Cor. 9.1–12.
[3] Cf. I Tim. 3.1–13.
[4] See ch. IV.
[5] Or 'fruit'.
[6] *Misthos*, 'pay'.

apart from works; and in spite of his insistence that the directing power of community and individual is now the Spirit, Paul retains and firmly stresses the idea that each man, including those within the Church, will be judged by what he has done.[1] The practical value of this expectation as an encouragement was not absent from Paul's mind. Beyond this, as in the Synoptic Gospels, the retention of the idea of 'reward' or 'pay' signified the certainty of the reward, rather than the measure of deserving. It is a way of expressing the dependability of God.[2] From another point of view, the conception of reward points to the element of continuity between this life and the life to come; this aspect of the idea of reward is shown in the use, for reward, of the term, 'final outcome'.[3] In the third place, the conception of a final assize, at which each individual comes before the judgment of God, expresses Paul's understanding of the permanent nature of personality, and in particular his intense awareness of himself. His own activity has significance in the coming, eternal world. This is particularly apparent in his bold use of the term 'boasting'. He speaks of being able to 'boast face to face with God'.[4]

All these elements are present in the use of the term 'pay'.[5] While salvation itself is a gift, and this fact is sometimes expressed by clear rejection of the word 'reward',[6] and while 'reward' is once used in a derogatory sense,[7] there still remains an appropriateness in the term 'pay' or 'reward', because it is necessary for man's labour to achieve real and permanent results.

It is to be observed that Paul does not entirely reject the conception of individual rewards for individual acts. This conception of reward was a marked feature of rabbinic Judaism.[8]

[1]Rom. 2.6–11, of men generally; I Cor. 4.4–5; II Cor. 5.10, of Christians.
[2]'God is faithful', I Cor. 1.9; cf. I Cor. 10.13; II Cor. 1.18; I Thess. 5.24.
[3]*Telos*; Rom. 6.21–23; II Cor. 11.15. The dependability of God appears on the negative side in the conception of 'wrath', which is almost a kind of impersonal process. Cf. Rom. 1.18; and Dodd, *Romans*, pp. 20–24.
[4]Rom. 15.17, as translated in Weiss, II, p. 562. Cf. also 'I would rather die than have anyone deprive me of my ground for boasting' (I Cor. 9.15).
[5]I Cor. 3.8, 14; cf. Rom. 4.4; I Cor. 9.17, 18.
[6]Rom. 6.21–23, where the 'wages' of sin are contrasted with the 'free gift' of God. Cf. Weiss, II, p. 561.
[7]Rom. 4.4.
[8]Bonsirven, *Le Judaïsme palestinien*, I, pp. 327–35, 504–11; II, pp. 53–69; G. F. Moore, *Judaism in the First Three Centuries of the Christian Era*, Cambridge, Mass., 1927–30, II, pp. 81–98.

Paul goes farther in ascribing individual rewards than Jesus is reported to have done in the Synoptic Gospels.[1] His reason for retaining the idea of individual reward is clearly the conviction that the acts of a man in this age have specific and permanent effects in the coming age. The clearest statement on this theme is found in I Cor. 3.10–15. Here the figure of various builders working on a building which will finally be tested with fire conveys the view that each man shall receive a specific reward in accordance with the nature of his work. As is usually the case with Paul, the metaphor is developed in a somewhat confusing way, which makes it doubly difficult to see clearly how he fits the inherited teaching into his new framework of thought. In any case, the fact of differential reward is clearly stated, and the passage throughout insists strongly on individual responsibility.[2] The testing of a man's work is a different thing from the question of his acceptance by God, for even the man who builds poorly will himself be saved.[3] The essential reason for retaining the conception of individual 'pay' is the conviction that man's activities are not passing and negligible, but can in some way affect the condition of that future existence into which man is called by God.

Thus the resulting picture is: man is responsible, and though he cannot effect his own salvation, his activities do have, within the Church of Christ, real and permanent results. In this present age, in tension between the old and new, the results may be real and cumulative; in the age to come, the final outcome of man's activities will be the recognition by God of the things which each man has done. Each man's achievements will thus be taken up into the new order. 'In the Lord your labour is not in vain.'[4] This practical reminder at the end of the long discussion of the resurrection shows the essential connexion between the two orders. Paul recognizes the ambiguity of the present existence. In spite

---

[1]References to individual reward for specific acts are not frequent in the teaching of the Synoptic Gospels. But cf. Matt. 5.19; 10.41; Luke 7.47; 12.47–8, and Amos N. Wilder, *Eschatology and Ethics in the Teaching of Jesus* (revised ed.), New York, 1950, pp. 88–9; H. J. Cadbury, *Jesus, What Manner of Man?* New York, 1947, p. 115.

[2]Robertson and Plummer, *I Corinthians*, pp. 64 f.

[3]I Cor. 3.15. A similar distinction is made in I Cor. 5.5, where Paul envisages the ultimate salvation of a man whose 'flesh' is 'delivered to Satan for destruction'.

[4]I Cor. 15.58.

of the fact that the new age is, in part, already present with the presence of Christ, there is no guarantee of success. The typical situation of the worker for Christ is that which he describes when he says, 'But I will stay in Ephesus until Pentecost, for a wide door for effective work has opened to me, and there are many adversaries.'[1] Here one works, and works in expectation of achieving results. And the results achieved bear a relation to the ultimate 'results' in a future order. The work constantly takes the form of facing opposition, so that there can be no proof in advance of the success of a specific task. Yet the very exhilaration with which Paul faces opposition shows that he is by no means a pessimist about the possibility of overcoming it. His hope is that work in which he is engaged will grow and increase in a very concrete way.

So far the discussion of Paul's view of work has treated man as a responsible agent, producing results by his own activities. This is one of Paul's ways of speaking. Yet he speaks also in a different way, in which it becomes apparent that the real force working in the Church of Christ and its individual members is God, or the Spirit of God, or Christ.

Often Paul speaks of the activity of God in terms of the 'Spirit'.[2] His own activity is not just *his* activity, but is carried on 'in demonstration of the Spirit and power'.[3] The consequences of his activities witness to this.[4] The work of the Spirit is not merely miraculous, but signifies more generally that in Paul's work one encounters God at work. A double movement, accentuating both God's activity and also human responsibility and even satisfaction in achievement appears also in reference to the central 'activity' of salvation: 'Work out your own salvation with fear and trembling; for God is at work in you, both to will and to work for his good pleasure.'[5] Likewise the concrete activities of the Church are the gift of God's grace. An example is the offering of the Gentile churches for Jerusalem.[6] The same double

[1] I Cor. 16.8–9.
[2] Rom. 8; Gal. 5.22–24.
[3] I Cor. 2.4–5.
[4] I Thess. 1.5.
[5] Phil. 2.12f.
[6] II Cor. 8.1. Cf. H. Lietzmann, *An die Korinther I, II* (HNT 9), 4th ed., supplemented by W. G. Kümmel, Tübingen, 1949, p. 133.

activity appears again when Paul compares himself to Apollos. He and Apollos are gardeners; God energizes the process of growth. 'I planted, Apollos watered, but God gave the growth.'[1] The untranslatable shift from aorist ('planted', 'watered') to imperfect ('gave the growth') emphasizes the point that God was continually at work in the whole process, including the planting and watering.[2] The point of the whole passage is that it is God, and not Paul and Apollos, who is really responsible for what has been done among the Corinthians. Yet even this section which so strongly stresses God's action, and states that the planter and waterer are 'not . . . anything', goes on to say that these workers will none the less receive their wages.[3] Similarly, he says of his work as an apostle, 'I worked harder than any of them, though it was not I, but the grace of God which is with me.'[4] Elsewhere he speaks of 'what Christ has wrought through me'.[5] The churches themselves, the fruit of his work and of the work of others, are really something that God has made.[6] Bertram believes that Paul elevated this new work of God to the level of a 'new creation': 'The establishment of the Christian community corresponds to the creation of the world, here as there is a work of God which takes place through the Word (the Spirit).'[7]

So strongly does Paul emphasize the fact that the inward energy of all effective work is God, so strongly does he feel that God is using him, Paul, as an instrument, that it is a noteworthy fact that Paul seldom speaks of God as doing *work*. The verb 'work' never takes 'God' or 'Christ' for its subject, while the related term 'achieve, produce' takes each of these subjects only once.[8] The

---

[1] I Cor. 3.6.
[2] Robertson and Plummer, *op. cit.*, p. 57.
[3] I Cor. 3.7–8.
[4] I Cor. 15.10.
[5] Rom. 15.18.
[6] 'The work of God', Rom. 14.20. Cf. Sanday and Headlam, p. 392; H. Leitzmann, *An die Römer* (HNT 8), 4th ed., Tübingen, 1933, p. 117. In the phrase 'God's building' (I Cor. 3.9), however, the genitive is simply possessive; cf. I Cor. 3.16 f.
[7] Bertram, *TWNT*, II, 640.
[8] *Ergazomai* ('work'), used eighteen times, including once in Ephesians, has a personal (human) subject in every occurrence but one. *Katergazomai* ('produce'), used twenty-one times including once in Ephesians, is used about equally with personal and impersonal (sin, law, etc.) subjects, showing that it is not closely associated with man's work.

noun 'work', which may mean work in the sense of the activity
or in the sense of the product, is usually but not always used of
man's work.[1] The 'work of the Lord' or 'of Christ' means work
done for Christ; the subject is clearly human worker.[2]

The hesitancy to speak of God as doing 'work' is probably due
in part to the element of effort in human work. The difficult
struggle of human labour does not appear to Paul to be an
appropriate metaphor with which to describe God's activity. The
noun and verb 'labour' are never used with God directly as the
subject, and these are the terms which most emphasize the element of laboriousness.[3]

In addition Paul hesitates to speak of God's 'work' because he
prefers to use terms which suggest that God's activity goes on at
a different level from that of man. God's activity is the essential
energy of man's work, if man's work is to be productive. But the
relationship between God's activity and that of man is not
parallel. This can be seen in Paul's reluctance to use the term
'fellow-worker'[4] of the relationship between God and man. As
stated above, Paul often used this term to refer to those who were
doing the same sort of work that he was.[5] There are several places
in which the term may indicate a co-operation between God and
man, but in these cases the meaning of the term is dubious.

One of these doubtful passages is found in the course of Paul's
discussion of his relationship to Apollos. In the conclusion of
this section, Paul remarks, 'For we are fellow workmen for God;
you are God's field, God's building.'[6] Paul and Apollos are
God's servants; they are doing his work. At bottom the building
of the Church is God's achievement. Yet Paul and Apollos will
receive their pay for their part in the work. In summing up, what
Paul says of himself and Apollos is literally, 'We are God's
fellow-workers.'[7] Lietzmann, and Robertson and Plummer interpret

[1]'Work' (*ergon*) is used of God's work in Rom. 14.20 (cf. p. 56 n. 6). In the
LXX, *ergon* or *erga theou* are very common. God is often associated indirectly
with man's work; cf. II Thess. 2.17; Phil. 1.6; Eph. 2.10.
[2]I Cor. 15.58; 16.10.
[3]But cf. I Cor. 15.10.
[4]*Synergos.*
[5]See above, p. 46.
[6]I Cor. 3.9; see p. 56.
[7]*Ibid.*, RV; the Greek is *theou gar esmen synergoi.*

this to mean 'workers with God',[1] while Bauer and Moffatt, like Goodspeed and RSV, hold that the phrase means 'workers together for God'.[2] The context appears to suggest the latter interpretation, for the point which Paul wishes to stress is not the authority of Apollos and himself as collaborators with God, but the fact that there is no division between him and Apollos. That God and man each contributed to the growth of the Church may be granted, from Paul's point of view; that he intended this by the phrase 'God's fellow-workers' is doubtful.

Another passage in which the same term appears is found in I Thess. 3.2. Here there is no doubt as to the meaning of the term. Timothy according to one text is called a 'fellow-worker with God'. This could scarcely be taken to mean 'a fellow-worker who belongs to God' in view of the clear parallel, 'my fellow-worker'.[3] The problem is simply the question of the correct text. From the point of view of rational criticism there is much to commend that Western form of the text which refers to Timothy as a worker with God. This text is adopted by Dibelius and Frame, though it is rejected by Robertson and Plummer, and by the principal modern English translations.[4] The textual evidence is strong if taken by itself.[5] But the evidence is difficult to interpret, since the various transcribers may not have been sensitive to the theological implications of the readings in the ways we suppose them to have been. Thus while it is the case that the study of the passage in isolation from others suggests a probability in favour of the reading 'a fellow-worker of God', it must be affirmed that this passage stands almost by itself and the text is at best uncertain. The reference to Timothy as a fellow-worker of God is all the more striking in view of the way in which Paul studiously avoids calling Timothy an apostle.[6] It is possible that Paul refers to men as fellow-workers of God in this passage and in the reference to

[1]Lietzmann, *An die Korinther*, p. 15; Robertson and Plummer, *op. cit.*, pp. 58 f.
[2]W. Bauer, *Griechisch-deutsches Wörterbuch*, 5th ed., Berlin, 1958, *s.v.*; Moffatt, *I Corinthians*, p. 39.
[3]Rom. 16.21, etc.
[4]Martin Dibelius, *An die Thessalonicher I, II: An die Philipper* (HNT 11), 3rd ed., Tübingen, 1937, p. 16; J. E. Frame, *Thessalonians* (ICC), Edinburgh, 1912, pp. 126 f.
[5]See the evidence in Dibelius and Frame, *ibid.*
[6]Cf. II Cor. 1.1.

himself and Apollos. In any case the striking fact is that he seldom does so, and that the references themselves are ambiguous in one way or another.

In another passage the verb from the same root is used, and here the probability seems to be on the other side, and the passage to say that God and man work together. 'Working together with him, then, we entreat you not to accept the grace of God in vain.'[1] The verb is simply 'working together',[2] and the context strongly suggests that 'God' be supplied.[3] For in the previous paragraph Paul speaks of himself as an 'ambassador for Christ', and he beseeches on 'behalf of Christ, God making his appeal through us'. Here, then, the term suggests the meaning 'working with God'.[4]

The striking fact is that these passages are so few and in every case somewhat ambiguous, as a detailed examination of them has shown. Paul was very cautious in speaking of God and man as working together. None the less, there is a very real 'synergism' in Paul's thought. When he thinks of the change in the individual person's status before God, and of the consequent inward change in his personality, through the presence of the Spirit, he speaks of God's activity. This realm cannot be mastered by man, even though the self must respond. On the other hand, when he thinks of the existence and growth of the Christian community, a visible yet eschatological reality, he speaks of the activity of God and of

[1] II Cor. 6.1.
[2] *Synergountes.*
[3] As it has been, in one way or another, in the RSV, and in Goodspeed's and Moffatt's translations. Cf. also A. Plummer, *II Corinthians* (ICC), Edinburgh, 1915, p. 189; Allan Menzies, *The Second Epistle to the Corinthians*, London, 1912, p. 45; Jean Héring, *II Corinthiens* (CNT 8), Paris, 1958, p. 55.
[4] The verb 'work together' (*synergein*) occurs elsewhere in Paul only in I Cor. 16.16 and in Rom. 8.28. In the former passage, where it is associated with *kopian* ('labour') the probability is that it refers to co-operation within the church. In Rom. 8.28, many modern interpreters reject the meaning, 'all things work together for good', (AV), in favour of a more theocentric interpretation: 'in everything God works for good with those who love him' (RSV). One form of the text supplies 'God', but God can be understood as subject of the verb in any case. But it is not typical of Paul to speak of God working with man. Cf. Adolf Schlatter, *Gottes Gerechtigkeit*, Stuttgart, 1935, pp. 281–2. Since the sentence probably comes to Paul as a traditional formulation (Otto Michel, *Der Brief an die Römer*, Göttingen, 1957, p. 180), the meaning, 'all things work together for good', may be accepted as a traditional formulation.

man. Here, in the realm of the building of the Church, is the realm of 'synergism'. Naturally the boundary between the two areas is a somewhat artificial one. The self cannot be changed unless there is a Church and preachers,[1] nor can the Church grow without the Spirit of Christ.[2] The two moments are clearly expressed together: 'All this is from God, who through Christ reconciled us to himself and gave us the ministry of reconciliation . . . So we are ambassadors for Christ, God making his appeal through us.'[3] God is at work, and has chosen to work through men. It would be truer to Paul's thought to say that all real human work is God's work than to say that God and man work together. As Bertram says,

> But the time of salvation re-establishes the situation in conformity to the creation; all work of men is the activity of God through men . . . For the believing Christian, the good works which meet him in life are never merely human work, but God's work through the hand of man.[4]

OTHER WORK IN THE CONTEXT OF THE CHRISTIAN COMMUNITY

A study of what Paul says about other sorts of work within the context of the Church shows that for him work done clearly and consciously in response to the divine command supplies the model for all real work.

A point of linkage between the work which explicitly furthers the divine purpose and what we might call 'ordinary' work is provided by Paul's own working for a living. It was his usual custom to work in a 'sweat-shop' trade and to carry on his missionary activity in his 'spare time'.[5] He took great pride in

---

[1]Rom. 10.14–15.
[2]Gal. 5.25; Rom. 8.9.
[3]II Cor. 5.18, 20.
[4]Bertram, *TWNT*, II, 649. Bertram, however, exaggerates when he says that the conviction of God's presence completely displaces a concern for human achievement. In discussing Phil. 1.22 ('If it is to be life in the flesh, that means fruitful labour for me') he remarks, 'Even here there is lacking at least for Paul every thought of his own achievement (*Leistung*) and its consequences' (*ibid.*, 640).
[5]Paul was a *skēnopoios*, according to Acts 18.3. By derivation this means 'tentmaker' (RSV, Goodspeed). Cadbury and Lake, Haenchen, and Moffatt's translation prefer 'leatherworker', on the basis of some early versions and early commentaries. Cf. H. J. Cadbury and Kirsopp Lake on Acts 18.3, in

this work, but what he writes shows no concern with its aspect of craftsmanship. Paul has no interest in work for its own sake, and little concern for the relation of work to the sub-human creation. The aspect of work as art, concerned with the 'stuff' which is worked, must find guidance elsewhere than from Paul. He worked to support himself. Apparently almost alone, he insisted on working instead of receiving support which was recognized as the right of the apostle or missionary.[1] He wanted financial freedom from the churches, his purpose being, as he said, not to 'put an obstacle in the way of the gospel of Christ'.[2] The characteristic motive of action in the new community— concern for the other and the weaker—leads Paul to set himself apart from the already-established practice of accepting financial support, and his work becomes part of his vocation as a whole.[3] Though there is no interest in work for its own sake, Paul's attitude towards his work reflects his Pharisaic background and stood in sharp contrast to much Greek thought, in that he saw physical work as a normal aspect of obedience to God.

Just as the special case of Paul shows work for a living taken up into the response of the whole self to the powers of the new age met in Christ, so, too, the Christian normally finds that obedience to Christ in the new community entails the continuance or the undertaking of his appropriate form of work. The very decision to separate oneself from the old aeon and accept its misunderstanding and persecution leads also to the acceptance of the demand to work, externally the same demand as that of common-sense morality, but now viewed from the perspective of self-denying concern for the other. Thus, 'to work with your own hands' is derived from 'love one another',[4] just as the humble character of Paul's own labour, 'working with his own hands', is a sign of the paradoxical position of the highest vocation, the apostleship, which appears to men as a pitiful 'spectacle'.[5]

Beginnings IV, p. 223, and E. Haenchen, *Die Apostelgeschichte*, Göttingen, 1959, p. 470. Whatever the exact nature of his work, it is clear from his own comments that it meant long hours of heavy drudgery. Cf. Weiss, I, pp. 185 f.

[1] I Cor. 9.1–18; II Thess. 3.7–9; Bienert, *Die Arbeit*, p. 300.
[2] I Cor. 9.12.
[3] I Cor. 9.22–23; II Cor. 6.3–10; 11.25–29.
[4] I Thess. 4.9–12.
[5] I Cor. 4.8–12.

Within the context of the new community, which already tastes the powers of the new age, the appropriate ethical motivation is free, self-forgetting love. Yet in the area of work as in several other areas, Paul finds that patterns from the old age can be, indeed must be, taken up into the life which anticipates the new, to be the vehicles through which the new relation of love expresses itself.[1]

Thus, each member must support himself.[2] Service to the community itself is the outstanding work of every Christian.[3] Paul's urging that Christians work so as to make a good impression on outsiders, finds its ground in the task of the community to commend its faith to others, while at the same time it shows how the new community takes up and gives meaning to a function of man in the world.[4]

In this sphere as elsewhere, Paul does not attempt to justify the Christian's work as valuable in itself. Because work may express the motive of love, because it may prevent one's becoming a burden to others, because in it one may dispel misapprehensions of non-Christians, work is necessary and meaningful. The same would apply to the work within the home as to the work of the wage-earner.

The social setting of work is taken for granted by Paul. Not only has he no desire to transform it; he holds that in this world the Christian's witness will normally be expressed in humility and obedience within the accepted patterns, whether to the government,[5] or to the husband, father, or master.[6] His orientation is not one of resignation, however; on the contrary, he expects all believers to be so completely absorbed in devotion to Christ and to the new community that their conformity to social patterns will be only incidental, while their real energy will be devoted to filling these relationships with the personal meaning of love.[7]

If, as often happens, the members of Paul's churches failed to rise to the level to which he challenged them, Paul could appeal to

[1] I Cor. 7, with its emphatic affirmation that marriage may be such a vehicle, represents an important and closely-related parallel.

[2] I Thess. 4.9-12; II Thess. 3.7-9; Bienert, *op. cit.*, p. 365.

[3] Cf. I Cor. 16.2; Bienert, *ibid.*; in Phil. 2.25-30, the service of the Philippians for Paul is the 'work of Christ'.

[4] I Thess. 4.10-12; cf. II Cor. 8.21; Col. 4.5.

[5] Rom. 13.1-7.

[6] Col. 3.18-4.1.

[7] I Cor. 7.1-7, on marriage; cf. more generally Gal. 5.13-24.

them and threaten them in terms of traditional and practical reasons for doing their work.[1] Such an acknowledgement of the necessity of establishing an objective form of Christian obedience leads to the creation of formalized patterns of teaching about the obligations of believers in their various stations. Such passages appear in Colossians and Ephesians, as well as elsewhere in the New Testament.[2] These formalizations of the duty of work ground a Christian's performance of his work directly in obedience to Christ,[3] and testify to the completeness with which the early Church absorbed all the activities of its members into the new orientation of faith.

Ordinary daily tasks are thus absorbed in the collective obedience of the community of Christ, and because they may all reflect the Christian's faith and obedience, they participate in the stretching-forward to the new age which is more obviously characteristic of Paul's own work. Of each functioning member of the Church it can be said, in the first place of his activities explicitly for the community, but by extention to all that he does in so far as it reflects his obedience to Christ, 'Be steadfast, immovable, always abounding in the work of the Lord, knowing that in the Lord your labour is not in vain.'[4]

Work in its everyday sense is not a divine 'vocation' for Paul except as it can have meaning in the context of that work which is *the* divine vocation, namely the work of communicating the gospel. The latter is the true vocation of every Christian, though not all perform it by preaching or proclamation.[5] When Paul urges each Christian, whether slave or free, to remain in the 'state in which he was called',[6] the 'state' (RSV) is literally the 'calling' (AV, RV); but Paul regularly uses this term only for the calling into the Christian life. Hence here we have either an abridged statement meaning 'the position in which he received his calling', or a shift of emphasis to the point that far more important than his external

[1] I Thess. 4.11-12; 5.14; II Thess. 3.6, 11-13.
[2] Col. 3.18-4.1; Eph. 6.5-9; cf. I Tim. 6.1-2; Tit. 2.9-10; I Peter 2.18-25; Richardson, *Doctrine of Work*, pp. 40-45; Martin Dibelius, *An die Kolosser, Epheser, an Philemon* (HNT 12), 3rd ed., revised by Heinrich Greeven, Tübingen, 1953, pp. 48-50.
[3] 'You are serving the Lord Christ,' Col. 3.24.
[4] I Cor. 15.58.
[5] Cf. Rom. 12.3-8.
[6] I Cor. 7.20.

station is his remaining in his true position of Christian, into which he has been called by Christ.[1]

A comparison with work as understood by the Essenes (here taken to include the Qumran community) is instructive in showing two contrasting eschatological interpretations of work.[2] In both cases one finds that work is lifted out of a merely traditional or moralistic setting and justified in relation to eschatological action. But among the Essenes the interpretation takes the form of a sanctification of a given social form of work, while in Paul the external social form is almost inconsequential. The Essene emphasis on agriculture[3] represents in their time a withdrawal to an ideal past not unlike the earlier nomadic emphasis of the Rechabites.[4] In both cases a given form of community, known from the past, serves as a vehicle for a protest against and withdrawal from the present evil age. While the Essenes no doubt did not adhere strictly to the agricultural pattern,[5] the whole project of erecting a pure and separate community which was total in its organization was in its Essene form strongly centred on the emphasis on a particular form of work. Paul's understanding of work was equally 'total', yet to him the external form is indifferent. The difference springs from the heightened awareness of eschatological action in Paul. For the Essenes, the expectation of God's coming act demands withdrawal from present evil[6] while in Paul the present activity of God in Christ offers the believer a power with which he can participate in activities in the world as worker, master, or slave, and yet give new meaning to these actions as they become functions of his new purposes derived from Christ. Thus in contrast to the Essenes Paul had a very much less obviously definable pattern by which to give meaning to work, since he held that under the influence of the Spirit, any work can find meaning if the worker's energies are directed to the Christian fellowship, and spring from the presence of Christ.

[1]Richardson, *op. cit.*, pp. 35–39; J. Héring, *I Corinthiens* (CNT 7), Paris, 1949, pp. 54–55; Bienert, *op. cit.*, pp. 339–40.
[2]Cf. the discussion in Bienert, *op. cit.*, pp. 153–7.
[3]Josephus, *Ant.* 18. 1.5.
[4]Cf. Jer. 35.1–19.
[5]See the instructive discussion of W. R. Farmer, 'The economic basis of the Qumran community', *Theologische Zeitschrift* XI (1955), 295–308.
[6]'Manual of Discipline', v. 1–7 (Gaster, *Scriptures*, p. 56).

SUMMARY

In summary, Paul's deepest understanding of man's work is that God, in his great task of saving men, has chosen to act through the work of men. Paul knows himself drawn into the purpose of God, and believes that what he does is really God's achievement. Yet the presence of God's (or Christ's) activity in his activity does not lessen his sense of individuality or responsibility. He knows himself to be achieving results which are concrete and visible, and he hopes that these will continue and will, by the work of others, become of even greater effect. He appeals to his success as a sign that God is working through him. Yet he holds that his work cannot really be measured by its success or failure in achieving visible results. For his work has value in the sight of God, and its ultimate result will be tested by God and rewarded. Thus his work has relevance both to the advance of the gospel and to the indescribable new order which God alone can establish.

Similarly, each believer's work is drawn into the sphere of the new community; he works for it in whatever his appropriate capacity may be, as assigned by the Spirit,[1] and his secular work, while never important in itself, nevertheless contributes to the maintenance of the community and provides a vehicle for the expression of the believer's faith and love. While Paul shows no interest in justifying work by appeal to a doctrine of its place in the created order, he can and does appeal to traditional ethical teaching about the value and necessity of work. Although such an appeal from Paul's perspective represents an elementary teaching for 'babes', it is an anticipation of a move to ground the value and meaning of work more extensively in the created order, that became of more importance as the intensity of absorption in the new community became less all-compelling. For Paul, it is the present eschatological gift of faith and the Spirit, and the forward-looking eschatological reference of work, that give it meaning. As men are caught up into the on-going purpose of God, which in his own time reached so critical a juncture, their work becomes no longer their own work, but God's, and so bears fruit for the final consummation of God's purpose.

[1] I Cor. 12.4–11.

IV

PROGRESS, GROWTH, AND PERFECTION

A QUESTION left open by the study of Paul's view of work was
the extent to which the effects of work can be expected to continue and grow. At times Paul speaks of work as increasing in its
effects, and the vigour with which he prosecutes his task suggests
that he did expect real and cumulative results. Yet he also shows
a clear awareness of the opposition to his work, and of the
consequent contingency with respect to permanent or cumulative
results in this order. It remains, therefore, to examine the conceptions of growth, progress, and perfection as they appear in the
message of Paul, in order to see whether these are used in ways
which complement the conception of work.

In the first place, growth and development are conceptions
which do not bulk large in Paul's thought. He is so firmly convinced that there is an unlimited resource at hand in the Spirit of
Christ, that he does not give close attention to questions of
growth, either the growth of character of the individual, or the
growth of the Church as an institution. As Johannes Weiss
remarks,

> . . . the idea of training and practical guidance as to what should
> be done if one would become more and more the master of one's
> own mind, so strongly in evidence in the Stoics, is almost wholly
> wanting in Paul. . . . The deepest reason for this deficiency is
> clear: even as an ethical teacher Paul is primarily a Spirit-filled man.[1]

Nevertheless, the necessity for growth in both individual and
community is clearly recognized, as can be seen from an examination of the terms used to describe it.

Change in itself is a neutral conception for Paul, and not of
great interest to him.[2] Duration, continuing in a state, comes more

[1] Weiss, II, pp. 576 f.
[2] *Allassein* (to change), used four times, means twice the change to a new
kind of body at the resurrection ('. . . we shall be changed', I Cor. 15.51-2),
and once the exchange of God's glory for images (Rom. 1.23, quoting

frequently into his practical exhortations than does change.[1] Paul was well aware of the fact of decisive change, but usually refers to changes in terms which specify their concrete content.[2]

PROGRESS

In spite of his comparative lack of interest in this aspect of life, Paul's comments on growth reveal that he has some characteristic things to say about it. One set of terms used for growth is the verb and noun 'to progress' and 'progress'.[3] The verb means literally 'to cut one's way forward' and was commonly used to refer to progress on a journey. These words for progress emphasized one's own application, and they were particularly applied to moral or intellectual progress, especially among the Stoics. The noun might consequently mean 'proficiency' as well as 'progress'; while in common parlance another meaning was simply 'success' or 'prosperity'.[4] Commonly applied by the Stoics to the advance made by discipline in an individual's life, the term 'progress' could also be used to describe progress in a joint endeavour—a reminder that within a limited sphere something akin to the idea of progress was not unknown to antiquity.[5] Paul uses this typically Greek term a number of times.[6] He speaks of his own 'progress in Judaism' in his early days.[7] Referring to the present, he speaks of the progress of the gospel, which was objectively manifest even though the motives for preaching were not in this case wholly sincere.[8] He expresses the hope that his activity will

---

Ps. 106.20 [105.20]), and once simply the 'change of tone' which Paul would like to adopt toward the Galatians (Gal. 4.20). *Epistrephein* (to turn) means twice to turn to God (II Cor. 3.16; I Thess. 1.9), and once to turn back from God (Gal. 4.9).

[1]Cf. in the moral sphere, *hypomonē* (endurance), Rom. 2.7, etc., and in the life of the Church, the continuance of *paradosis* (tradition), I Cor. 11.2; II Thess. 2.15; cf. I Cor. 11.23; 15.3, and *synētheia* (custom), I Cor. 11.16; cf. also, for continuing Paul's pattern of teaching, I Cor. 4.17; 7.17.

[2]E.g., 'to believe', 'to be justified'.

[3]*Prokoptein, prokopē.*

[4]Liddell and Scott, *s.v.* § I 2b; Preisigke, *s.v.*

[5]Epict., *Diss.* iii 6.1–4 discusses the question why there is no progress in the study of logic as there had been in the past.

[6]In the LXX 'progress' occurs only in Ecclus. 51.17; II Macc. 8.8. It is common in Philo.

[7]Gal. 1.14. In Rom. 13.12 this verb refers simply to the passage of time.

[8]Phil. 1.12.

assist the progress of the Philippians.[1] In one case the term applies to the 'gospel', in the other to the people. The thought is the same in both cases: the work of Paul and of others has resulted in a new and better situation.

Related in spirit to the conception of the individual's 'progress' are the athletic and military metaphors of which Paul makes considerable use. Like the conception of individual development, these metaphors are widely used in popular Greek morality, and were especially common in the Stoic diatribe.[2] In Paul's letters the moral struggle is not infrequently pictured in the form of an athletic contest. The athletic metaphors usually emphasize the strenuous moral exertion which is necessary for victory, though once the metaphor is used to state precisely the reverse.[3] Though he once uses the picture of the runner who falls behind in a race as a rebuke,[4] it is interesting that Paul most frequently applies the athletic metaphors to himself, picturing himself as a runner or boxer who devotes all his energies to winning the prize.[5] Sometimes the point of comparison is the concrete result which he wishes to obtain, sometimes the final reward; in either case the metaphor suggests the incompleteness of the present situation, either as to its actual results, or as to the inner character of the contestant. Except in the one case noted above, the race or contest always emphasizes the connexion between present effort and future results or reward.

Related to these metaphors are the references to life as a 'conflict'.[6] Weiss observes that these athletic metaphors connect with the ideal of testing and experience; that is, the seasoning of character by hardship and suffering.[7] Here, too, can be observed a kind of conception of growth of character.[8]

[1] Phil. 1.25.
[2] Paul Wendland, *Die urchristlichen Literaturformen* (HNT I 3), Tübingen, 1912, p. 356 n. 4.
[3] Rom. 9.16, 'So it depends not upon man's will or exertion, but upon God's mercy.' 'Man's . . . exertion' is literally 'of the runner'.
[4] Gal. 5.7.
[5] I Cor. 9.24–27; Gal. 2.2; Phil. 2.16; 3.12–14.
[6] Phil. 1.30; Col. 2.1; I Thess. 2.2; cf. the corresponding verb (participle) appears in I Cor. 9.25; Col. 1.29; 4.12, though it is not very apparent in translation.
[7] Weiss, II, p. 577.
[8] Rom. 5.3b–4, '. . . suffering produces endurance, and endurance produces character, and character produces hope . . .'

Closely related to the athletic metaphors are the military, but the latter are used in a wide variety of ways. For the ancient athlete was largely an individual contestant, and the metaphor is used by Paul, as by others, largely to suggest individual exertion. The soldier, however, was a figure who suggested other things besides the vigour of his fighting. In Paul he sometimes appears as an employee, and the pay which a soldier receives for his services is the point of comparison.[1] Most frequently, however, Paul compares the aid which comes from Christ, or God, to a soldier's weapon. Unlike the athlete, the soldier receives 'outside assistance', as Paul uses the metaphor. The weapons are 'the armour of light'.[2] They are 'not worldly but have divine power to destroy strongholds'.[3] They are the 'weapons of righteousness',[4] or 'the breastplate of faith and love, and for a helmet the hope of salvation'.[5] All of these pictures are ways of suggesting that the man who is 'in Christ' fights with more than his own resources. In the more fully developed metaphor of Ephesians, the struggle is against demonic powers.[6] Paul himself never makes explicit the element of conflict with the demonic world, in his use of military metaphors. He draws both from the Old Testament and from Hellenistic-Roman military traditions, as did the author of the 'War of the Sons of Light and the Sons of Darkness'.[7] But Paul does not interpret the struggle of God and the powers of darkness in an objective, speculative way, as often in the apocalyptic literature. Rather he transfers the metaphors of struggle into the life of the believer and of himself. This internalizing of the conflict is one of Paul's ways of communicating his awareness of the fact that God's historical action is not something external, but is now creating a reality in which the believer can participate. It is noteworthy that his military metaphors most clearly show their eschatological root when he speaks of his own function; he

[1] I Cor. 9.7; cf. Rom. 6.23, where the words 'wages' and 'free gift' are terms for payments to soldiers.
[2] Rom. 13.12.
[3] II Cor. 10.3–4 (of his own 'equipment').
[4] II Cor. 6.7.
[5] I Thess. 5.8.
[6] Eph. 6.10–17.
[7] Note the phrase 'helmet of salvation', Isa. 59.17; I Thess. 5.8. See Heinrich Greeven, in Martin Dibelius, *An die Kolosser, Epheser, an Philemon*, pp. 96–97; Gaster, *Scriptures*, pp. 267–72.

himself is engaged in a divine cosmic struggle as he faces his opponents in Corinth.[1] The association of military metaphors with the expectation of impending judgment reinforces the setting of the Christian struggle in the eschatological pattern. God is about to win a great victory; men are summoned to his standard (in both senses of the term!) and enlisted in his army which will win a great victory.[2] The advance which is under way is a struggle for Christ as well as for men,[3] and the believer's struggle finds its meaning in that it is directed to the same goal as Christ's.

GROWTH

A related conception, somewhat less sharply defined, is that of growth. In spite of the relatively infrequent appearance of this conception, Paul does refer to growth a number of times as a normal process in both individual and community. Paul expresses a hope for the growth of the 'faith' of the Corinthian Church, and this growth includes increased influence.[4] Again, speaking of the Corinthian contribution to Jerusalem, he refers to the increase of the 'harvest of your righteousness', i.e., the results of generosity.[5] Here God is the cause of the growth, and the same is the case in the metaphor in which he compares the Corinthians to a growing garden, and himself and Apollos to the gardeners.[6] In Colossians Paul speaks of the growth of 'the gospel', and here again growth is associated with increasing effects.[7] A few verses later the same verbs which had been used to describe the gospel's growth are applied to the growth of the Colossians themselves in respect to their knowledge of God.[8] In Colossians, which is here followed by Ephesians, there appears the picture of the Church as a harmoniously growing body. Again comes the emphasis that

[1] II Cor. 10.3–4.
[2] Rom. 13.11–14; I Thess. 5.1–11.
[3] 'For he must reign until he has put all his enemies under his feet', I Cor. 15.25.
[4] II Cor. 10.15.
[5] II Cor. 9.10.
[6] I Cor. 3.5–9; see above, p. 56.
[7] 'Bearing fruit and growing', Col. 1.6.
[8] Col. 1.10. Increase is also frequently expressed by the verbs *perisseuein* (to be or have more; used thirty-seven times), and *pleonazein* (to be or make abundant; used seven times).

the energy and direction of growth come from God.[1] Other
metaphors which might suggest growth are drawn from agriculture. In these, however, the point of comparison is usually the
sowing and harvesting, applied to the judgment. This metaphor is
used by Paul, as it had been frequently before him, to suggest the
dependable outcome of the process of life. The element of growth
is not really the point of the metaphor, but rather the element of
waiting for the harvest.[2] Growth is a prominent feature of the
agricultural metaphor only in the picture of Paul and Apollos as
gardeners caring for the Church which God makes grow.

A metaphor related to growth is that of 'building'. Paul speaks
of the Church as a building.[3] Here again, the growth of the building is in the background, and the stress falls on the present action
of the builders and its final testing. Only once in the various uses
of the metaphor of building is the thought of developing stages
prominent in the metaphor.[4] In Ephesians, however, the comparison is used to emphasize the process of growth of a building.[5]
In a more general way the words 'building' and 'to build' refer
to the growth of the Church. They become, in fact, almost
technical terms for 'church work'. Almost always these words are
applied to the building up of the Church, though they may also
be used of the individual.[6] The appearance of these terms shows
Paul's concern for the maintenance of the Church as a tangible
group, and he refers to his 'authority' given him by the Lord for

---

[1]'. . . the whole body . . . grows with a growth that is from God',
Col. 2.19; cf. Eph. 4.16. In Rom. 12.4–8 and I Cor. 12.12–26, the metaphor
of the body is used to suggest harmony in diversity, and the conception of
growth does not appear.

[2]Gal. 6.7–9. The 'harvest' was a standard figure in Jewish apocalyptic.
Cf. II (4) Esdras 9.17, 31, and H. L. Strack and P. Billerbeck, *Kommentar zum
Neuen Testament aus Talmud und Midrasch*, Munich, 1922–38, III, p. 578. In
II Cor. 9.6–12 the conception of growth, among others, is present in the
rather fluid metaphor. Other agricultural metaphors are found in I Cor.
9.7–12; 15.36–37; Rom. 11.16b–24. In none of these cases is growth the
point of comparison.

[3]I Cor. 3.9. Gaster, *Scriptures*, p. 254 n. 19, calls attention to the parallel
language of the Qumran commentary on Ps. 37, which he translates (p. 244)
'they have built for Him a congregation.'

[4]Rom. 15.20. In Gal. 2.18 he argues that he is not building up the things
which he tore down; in II Cor. 5.1, the 'building' is the resurrection body.

[5]Eph. 2.20–22.

[6]I Cor. 8.10 (of a wrong development).

building up the Church.[1] The impelling power which builds up, however, is love.[2] The great goal of the gifts of the Spirit is that they be directed to building up the Church, and not just to the ecstatic enjoyment of the individual.[3] In general, 'building up' means increasing the co-operative, peaceful harmony of the group and eliminating faction, quarrelling, and self-assertion. Increasing size or influence is not generally in mind.[4] Furthermore, the emphasis on 'building up' the Church did not mean a turning away from the eschatological interest toward a conception of growth in this order. As H. A. Guy observes, the apocalyptic hope was itself a potent force for building up the Church.[5]

PERFECTION

'Perfection' is a conception related both to growth and to progress. Paul speaks occasionally about the 'perfect' or 'mature' person, and while there has been considerable discussion about the meaning of this term, at least it is clear that 'perfection' is primarily an idea applied to the individual, not to the community.

Sometimes the *teleios* ('perfect') is contrasted with the child, suggesting that perfection may be considered the result of a process of growth, and that the term is best translated 'mature'.[6] The same contrast between the 'mature' and the child is clearly implied when Paul calls the Corinthians 'babes in Christ' in contrast to 'spiritual men'.[7] The contrast between 'children' and 'mature men' was a standard one in popular moral teaching, and suggested the experience, dependability, and ability to fulfil demands which are the mark of adult moral life.[8] Once more, the process of growth is present but in the background. The experience and ability of the mature person are the things which make the expression appropriate.

[1]II Cor. 10.8; 13.10; cf. 12.19.
[2]I Cor. 8.1.
[3]I Cor. 14. The noun and verb occur seven times in this chapter.
[4]Cf. previous note and the references on p. 71; and for 'to build', I Cor. 10.23; I Thess. 5.11; for 'building', Rom. 14.19; 15.2; cf. Eph. 4.12, 16, 29.
[5]H. A. Guy, *New Testament Prophecy*, London, 1947, p. 105; cf. I Cor. 14.4–5.
[6]I Cor. 2.6; 14.20; Phil. 3.15; Col. 1.28; 4.12; cf. Eph. 4.13.
[7]I Cor. 3.1; the 'spiritual men' are the 'perfect'; cf. I Cor. 2.6.
[8]Robertson and Plummer, *I Corinthians*, p. 35; Moffatt, *op. cit.*, pp. 27 f.; H. A. A. Kennedy, *St Paul and the Mystery-Religions*, London, 1913, p. 132, nd the references cited there.

Nevertheless, Paul well knew, as did the popular moral teachers, that the maturity of which he spoke was the result of a process. He did not lay down detailed plans of discipline, but he was keenly aware that not all had reached maturity, and he makes it his aim, he says, to 'present every man mature in Christ'.[1] Speaking of himself, he says that he is not 'already perfect', but presses on toward the goal.[2] Paul here speaks of maturity as the result of moral struggle and discipline, and here again he touches on another common use of the term.[3] The remarkable feature of 'maturity' in this section is the way in which Paul does not claim it for himself, but then refers to those who are already 'perfect', and commands them to engage in the same pursuit of the goal in which he is engaged.[4] Perhaps there is an implied rebuke here for those who claim perfection, as there is a rebuke for the claim of knowledge in I Corinthians.[5] But the same exhortation to the man who has already attained, to make further progress, is found in Stoic teaching.[6] The 'perfect' man in Paul's thought is thus best understood as the 'mature' man, the responsible adult who has experienced and is experiencing the full meaning of what it is to be 'in Christ'. Fundamentally such maturity is a gift of God.[7] But the gift must be appropriated by making the appropriate response.[8]

The above discussion has affirmed that perfection or maturity for Paul is the result of successive personal responses to the gift of Christ's Spirit. This interpretation of perfection as maturity attained by discipline appears to be justified by the contexts in which Paul uses the term. It should, however, be noted that at one time a considerable segment of scholarly opinion inclined

[1]Col. 1.28.
[2]Phil. 3.12; see above, p. 68.
[3]Philo, *Leg. alleg.* 3.159, cited by Kennedy, *op. cit.*, p. 133, contrasts 'the perfect' with 'the beginner' and 'the advancer'; cf. the other references in Kennedy, *ibid.*, and Charles Guignebert, 'Quelques remarques sur la perfection (*teleiōsis*) et ses voies dans le mystère paulinien', *RHPR* VIII (1928), 425.
[4]Phil. 3.15.
[5]I Cor. 8.1.
[6]Epict., *Enchir.* 51.1–2; cf. the phrase 'a mature man who is making progress' (*teleion kai prokoptonta*), *ibid.*, 51.2. Cf. Kennedy, *op. cit.*, p. 133.
[7]Phil. 3.12; 'I press on to make it my own, because Christ Jesus has made me his own.' Cf. II Cor. 5.18; Gal. 4.9; and R. N. Flew, *The Idea of Perfection in Christian Theology*, p. 68.
[8]Lietzmann, 'Todestaufe und christliche Ethik', *An die Römer*, pp. 65–8.

toward a different view. Richard Reitzenstein has noted that 'the perfect' was a technical term for the mystery-devotee, who by virtue of the infused divine spirit had access to the secrets of divine wisdom. He notes that Paul uses 'spiritual man' as a synonym for 'the perfect',[1] and that Paul associates the 'spiritual man' with knowledge of divine wisdom of a type not to be discussed among those who have not attained to this stage of religious experience.[2] From these parallels to mystery-cult langauge, Reitzenstein concluded that the terms 'perfect' and 'spiritual' both indicate primarily that transformation of substance which accompanied the infusion of divine spirit: '*Der pneumatikos ist überhaupt nicht mehr Mensch*'.[3] Specifically, Reitzenstein suggests that 'perfect' has the technical meaning, 'initiated'.[4]

Fully to discuss Reitzenstein's views would entail an examination of the conception of Spirit which cannot be undertaken here. While he is probably right in emphasizing that the word *teleios* ('perfect') had mystery-cult association for Paul and for his hearers,[5] it is doubtful that it had the technical sense, 'initiated'.[6] Reitzenstein is also correct in observing that Paul's language in speaking of the Spirit at times approaches the mystery terminology in which Spirit is felt to be a substance which fills or even replaces the self.[7] Yet a study of Paul's conception of Spirit would

---

[1] I Cor. 2.6; 3.1.

[2] *Ibid.*

[3] R. Reitzenstein, *Die hellenistischen Mysterienreligionen*, 3rd ed., Leipzig, 1927, p. 341.

[4] *Ibid.*, p. 338. Guignebert, *op. cit.*, 426, also holds that Paul's conception of perfection comes from the mysteries rather than from popular Greek moralism.

[5] This was already observed by Lightfoot, quoted by Kennedy, *op. cit.*, p. 135. Cf. J. B. Lightfoot, *Saint Paul's Epistles to the Colossians and to Philemon*, 9th ed., London, 1890, p. 168 (on Col. 1.28).

[6] Arndt and Gingrich (*s. teleios* §§ 2aβ, 2b; *teleioō* § 3) hold that this is the probable meaning in Phil. 3.15; Col. 1.28, and possibly I Cor. 2.6, and give a similar meaning to *teleioō* in Phil. 3.12. But *teleō*, not *teleioō*, is the verb commonly associated with mystery initiations; cf. Liddell and Scott, *s. teleō* § III. *Teleios* was clearly a mystery term, and connected with special knowledge; cf. *Tract. Herm.* 4.4. 'Such as have understood the proclamation and have been baptized of mind, these have partaken of knowledge (*gnosis*), and have become perfect (*teleioi*) men, having received mind.' But even in this passage it does not mean initiated in a technical sense, though this passage is often cited in support of that meaning.

[7] I Cor. 3.1–3; II Cor. 3.18; cf. Guignebert, *op. cit.*, 418 f.

show that he always refrains from carrying his Spirit-terminology to what were, from the mystery point of view, its logical conclusions.[1] He is held back by a strong sense of the 'I–thou' quality of the relationship which the Spirit establishes.[2] Likewise here, in speaking of perfection, the extent of mystery-cult association that the word has is probably rather slight, in view of the clear parallels in the papyri and in popular Stoicism to the meaning 'mature'. As it is found in the later gnostic writings, there was a sharp distinction between the 'perfect' and those who had no hope of ever attaining this state—a distinction quite foreign to Paul. Further, Paul emphasizes the element of moral struggle involved in the attainment of maturity.

In any case, perfection or maturity for Paul is primarily an individual matter. But even this concept, so strongly individualistic in its origins, is not left so by Paul. He speaks of love as the bond which 'binds everything together in perfect harmony'.[3] Love, which is itself the supreme gift of the Spirit, brings all together into a true community.[4]

CONCLUSION

Progress, growth, and perfection are not central conceptions in Paul's thought. Yet their place in his moral teaching indicates his recognition of the necessity for moral development in the individual. Characteristic of Paul, moreover, is the way in which he continually relates the growth of the individual to the community. Of the various conceptions discussed in this chapter the most markedly individualistic is that of 'perfection' or 'maturity'. Yet even here, Paul brings the concept into relation with the community. Similarly, the conception of 'progress', likewise individualistic in its background, becomes for Paul an appropriate term for the advance of the whole community, while a phrase like 'your progress'[5] cannot be said to apply either to the

[1]Paul never says that man becomes spirit, though he does become 'spiritual'. Cf. the Montanist prophetess Maximilla, cited in Reitzenstein, *op. cit.*, p. 318: 'I am word and spirit and power.'
[2]Weiss, II, pp. 470 f.
[3]Col. 3.14; cf. 'love is the link of the perfect life' (Moffatt).
[4]I Cor. 12.31; Gal. 5.22; cf. Flew, *op. cit.*, pp. 69 f.
[5]Phil. 1.25.

community or to the individual exclusively, so fully are the two brought together. Most clearly of all is the interplay of individual and community revealed in the conceptions of 'growth' and 'building up'. The growth of the individual requires harmonious integration into the group, and Paul expects that increasing harmony will increase the 'progress' or 'building up' of the group, including its increasing impact on outsiders.

As for the source of progress, Paul characteristically insists that God is the giver of all true growth, and also insists on whole-hearted moral endeavour. The Christian fights—with God's weapons. His perfection is something for which he must strive—yet it can result only from the possession of the Spirit which is God's gift. This element of Paul's teaching he felt to be distinct both from Judaism (with its works) and from popular pagan morality (with its emphasis on progress). The Stoic believed that he could 'develop' away from his shortcomings; Paul held that a decisive break with sin had to be made by God, and that then the Christian was free and responsible as he had never fully been before. His language is akin to that of the Stoics in his continual emphasis that growth, or progress, comes by conflict with opposing powers; it is akin to that of the mysteries in its indicating that the power which transforms life comes 'from the outside', from God. Yet his language also differs from both because he held that the divine reality encountered in Christ was not a substance, but a personal reality. The relationship between man and God is fundamentally 'prophetic' in form.[1]

The conceptions of growth, progress, and perfection are not closely connected with the relationship of man to history, since they are primarily expressions of the relation of the individual to himself, i.e., his own development. Yet the individual cannot become mature by himself. He grows as part of a community, and if other factors are equal, the community will grow by virtue of his growth. The 'growth' of the community is not primarily growth in size and influence, but these are not excluded from the building up of the Church. Paul's buoyant confidence was that the word of the Lord would 'speed and triumph' even in the present.[2] He thinks of change and development of the community,

[1]See pp. 105–11.
[2]II Thess. 3.1.

including concrete changes such as increasing size and influence, as to be expected.[1] Hence a constellation of conceptions which are principally oriented toward the individual nevertheless display, in Paul's use of them, his conviction that a visible growth of the churches is by no means impossible; on the contrary, it is to be expected, although it is also to be expected that such growth will come about only by conflict with opposing forces.[2]

What is lacking in Paul's comments about growth is any conviction that the results which are to be expected will be in any significant way permanently cumulative in this world. He sets no limits to the possibilities of the extension of God's purpose through the Church,[3] but on the other hand, he does not think of one individual's or group's development as becoming a foundation on which a succeeding time could build. It is not merely the expected shortness of the time which excludes interest in the possibility of a cumulative social growth of the Church. More important is the fact that although in one way cumulative results are expected—one person influences another—in another way the outcome is always threatened by the opposing forces, and has to be newly affirmed repeatedly in the decision of faith. Though some elements from the surrounding culture are taken up into the new community, Paul has no conception of the Church as a factor within culture, extending its influence by virtue of its being able to exert the same sort of force that other institutions exert. On the contrary, the Church is so different from any other human cultural group that it can only be set over against these groups, and it can only grow by negating the standards and powers that make for growth in the world.

Thus the conception of growth in Paul presents the same openness, or even ambiguity, that has been observed in connexion with the conception of work. Real results are obtainable in this world, and there is no note of hopelessness as Paul surveys his growing churches. Yet the growth which he envisages is strictly limited by the circumstances of the present era, and threatened

---

[1]Col. 1.6; 2.19; I Cor. 3.5–9.

[2]That there may be a relationship between the growth of the Church in this era, and the coming of the end, is suggested by the use of the apocalyptic conception of filling up the 'full number' of the elect (Rom. 11.25).

[3]Cf. esp. Rom. 11.

by opposing forces.[1] Historical growth, in so far as Paul touches on it, is not a process which can be expected to transform the whole of objective historical reality. Though the content which he gives to the idea of growth is distinctive, the formal pattern of growth in Paul is thus not essentially different from the limited pattern of growth and development which was seen to be possible by ancient philosophers and historians.[2]

[1]Preiss, 'The vision of history in the New Testament', *Life in Christ*, pp. 76–79.
[2]Gottlob Schrenk, 'Die Geschichtsanschauung des Paulus', *Jahrbuch der Theologischen Schule Bethel* III (1932), 62 n. 11.

V

PAUL AS APOSTLE

PAUL'S awareness of his place in God's purpose finds its most pointed expression in his understanding of himself as an apostle. This term is one which he found current in the Church, but made peculiarly his own—so much so that at certain points it is difficult to tell how the apostle was understood before and apart from Paul.

THE TERM

The Greek verbal adjective, *apostolos*, 'sent', 'the one sent', was not common, and its use was largely confined to naval and maritime affairs. Infrequently it was used in a more general way of persons sent to discharge a specified task.[1] Early Christian use of the term is related to the Hebrew *shalaḥ* (send), which often carried the meaning, 'to commission'.[2] Talmudic Hebrew has a noun, *shaliaḥ*, which appears in legal discussions as a technical term meaning 'agent' or 'delegate', a person sent not merely to carry out a command but to act as a responsible representative. The function of representative authority was expressed in the maxim, 'A man's agent (*shaliaḥ*) is like to himself.'[3] As representatives of God, Moses and the priests are designated by this term, but it does not seem to have been used for prophets, nor for Jewish missionaries. This limitation probably reflects an understanding of both prophets and missionaries which thought of them as speaking for God, not acting for him.[4]

There is, none the less, a clear and close parallel between the Hebrew and Greek terms in their general meaning of delegate or

---

[1]Herod., *Hist.* 1.21 ('ambassador'); K. H. Rengstorf, *Apostleship* (ET) (Bible Key Words), London, 1952, p. 2.

[2]E.g., Ex. 3.10 (God 'sends' Moses); Isa. 6.8; Jer. 1.7; 14.14, etc.

[3]Ber. 5.5; H. Danby, *The Mishnah,* Oxford, 1933, p. 6; cf. Rengstorf, *op. cit.,* p. 14.

[4]*Ibid.,* pp. 19–21. T. W. Manson, *The Church's Ministry,* London, 1948, pp. 38–47.

responsible representative. Paul uses the word *apostolos* twice in this general sense, and examples are found in other New Testament writings, in various specific applications.[1] The Greek term *apostolos* thus seems to have gained currency as a translation of the Hebrew *shaliaḥ* and its Aramaic equivalent, and to have indicated responsible representative character.

Whether or not *apostolos* was a current term for delegate in Greek-speaking Judaism is a question that has been much discussed; probably it was, though the only known instances are late.[2] In any case the time and place of adoption of the Greek expression do not vitally affect its meaning, while the varied use of the Greek word *apostolos* in the meaning of 'responsible representative' strongly indicates dependence on the corresponding Jewish term. The choice of this term is related to the fact that the verb *apostellein*, like the Hebrew *shalaḥ*, frequently indicated authorization.[3]

Though the scanty evidence summarized above indicates the origin of the Early Christian term *apostolos* in its meaning of 'delegate', there is no significant known antecedent for the specific term 'apostle of Christ', in which the term is set in the context of God's eschatological action. Here 'apostle' means 'authoritative representative of Christ', chosen by him to participate in a

---

[1] II Cor. 8.23, of the delegates who accompanied the gift to Jerusalem; Phil. 2.25, of Epaphroditus, who represented the Philippians; cf. John 13.16, 'Nor is he who is sent (*apostolos*) greater than he who sent him'; Heb. 3.1–2; Mark 6.30; cf. H. von Campenhausen, 'Der urchristliche Apostelbegriff', *Studia Theologica* I (1947), 101.

[2] Kirsopp Lake, 'The Twelve and the Apostles', in *Beginnings* V, pp. 49 f.; A. Harnack, *The Mission and Expansion of Christianity*, trans. J. Moffatt, 2nd ed., London, 1908, I, p. 330; H. Mosbech, '*Apostolos* in the New Testament', *Studia Theologica* II (1948), 188; G. Dix, 'The Ministry in the Early Church', *The Apostolic Ministry*, ed. K. E. Kirk, London, 1946, pp. 228 ff.; von Campenhausen, *op. cit.*, pp. 100 f. It is true that the term is scarcely known in its meaning 'delegate' in Jewish Greek of the New Testament period. Rengstorf, *op. cit.*, p. 11, cites Josephus, *Ant.* 1.146, where the text is doubtful, and *Ant.* 17.300. The word *apostolos* occurs once in the LXX, in a strongly verbal sense (I Kings 14.6), and once each in Aquila and Symmachus. Almost all of the extant references to Jewish *apostoloi* occur in Christian documents. But the term appears as a loanword in a Latin Jewish epitaph. Though this is late (fifth or sixth century), its use shows that the Greek word was used in Judaism; cf. Rengstorf, *op. cit.*, pp. 12–13; von Campenhausen, *op. cit.*, p. 101 n. 1.

[3] Rom. 10.15, and frequently in John and elsewhere.

process leading to the fulfilment of God's purpose, which is to create a 'new age'. This eschatological use of the term may stem from Jesus' sending out of his followers during his ministry, but it is also possible that the term only came into use with the resurrection-authorization of apostles.[1]

THE APOSTLE AS REMEMBERED

The Church looking back to its beginnings remembered the apostles mainly as administrative figures. The representative authority for which they were remembered was associated with the stabilization of the developing organization; they were thought of as vested with the right to direct both teaching and administration by their endowment direct from Christ. This administrative and regularizing conception of the apostolate rests in part on developments in second-century Christianity. The struggle with heresy, particularly gnosticism, drove the problem of ecclesiastical authority to the fore, and the result was the development of 'apostolic succession'. This might better be described as the episcopal succession, but it derived its name from its claim to represent and maintain in perpetuity the original, non-heretical, form of the Church and its doctrine. Thus the apostles came to be regarded as ecclesiastical authorities because their successors, the bishops, were such—old apostle was but new bishop writ large.[2] None the less, the Church also recognized the incompleteness of this ecclesiastical-legal interpretation, both by preserving and elaborating the memories of the apostles as proclaimers of the gospel (as in the apocryphal Acts), and even more strikingly, by the universal consent which reserved the term for an earlier time: even the Montanists did not claim to be or have apostles, for all their effort to recover the original eschatological message of the earliest Christian times.[3]

Though the struggle to attain some visible unity in the faith reached a peak of intensity in the second century, it was by no

---

[1] Apart from several references in Luke, Matt. 10.2 and one text of Mark 3.14, the only reference to the twelve as 'apostles' during the ministry of Jesus is Mark 6.30, which may indicate a temporary authorization for the mission from which they return. (Cf. Mark 6.7.)

[2] E.g., Ignatius, Mag. 7.1.

[3] E. Molland, 'Le développement de l'idée de succession apostolique', *RHPR* XXXIV (1954), 11.

means new to that time. The conception of the apostle as an ecclesiastical authority is already represented in Acts. It is from Luke-Acts above all that the Church derived the familiar idea that there were twelve apostles, and that they functioned as administrative and doctrinal authorities in Jerusalem, constituting a kind of court of appeal for difficult cases.[1] The limitation of the apostolate to the twelve is not rigorously carried out in Acts, since Paul and Barnabas are called apostles[2]—perhaps the author takes the term uncritically from a source, or possibly he is suggesting that Paul and Barnabas are 'delegates' of the Church, which would be close to making them 'apostles from men', the very thing that Paul so vigorously denies in Galatians.[3] It is also true that in Acts the apostles are not sole authorities for long, since James the Lord's brother soon makes his appearance and becomes the dominating figure in the Jerusalem Church, and since the 'elders' appear with the apostles. None the less, it is particularly to Acts that we owe the picture of the apostles as the original 'twelve', now endowed by Christ with a special right to rule the Church, even though this administrative power is nowhere defined by Luke.

PAUL THE APOSTLE

Paul too was very much concerned with the authority of the apostle—mainly in connexion with his own authority. Yet the framework of thought within which apostolic authority is viewed by Paul is very different from that of the later Church, which was striving to solve the problem of the continuity of faith in an organization existing in this world.

For Paul the apostle is an eschatological figure, charged by Christ with the immensely significant task of proclaiming the gospel and making it effective in the accomplishment of the divine purpose. Though he boldly asserts his authority, he does not primarily conceive this in relation to the maintaining of the Church as a continuing group, but with reference to his task of being the vehicle through whom God achieves a necessary stage

---

[1]Acts 2.42; 15.2, 22; 16.4, etc.
[2]Acts 14.4, 14.
[3]Gal. 1.1.

in his great work which has already, through Christ, in preliminary fashion neutralized the fabric of 'this world'.

It has long been recognized that Paul thought of himself as similar to or even superior to the focal Old Testament persons whom God had chosen to fulfil his purposes.[1] Like Jeremiah, he believed that God had set him apart before he was born.[2] The striking contrast between the old and new covenants in II Cor. 3 is extended beyond Paul—'we all with unveiled face beholding the glory of the Lord'.[3] But at the beginning of the chapter Paul's position as minister of the new covenant, in contrast to Moses as minister of the 'dispensation of death',[4] is pointed out in terms that indicate his standing higher in the fulfilment of God's purpose than Moses himself. Recent discussion has insisted that Paul's vocation grows from a clear pattern of eschatological expectation: Paul knows himself to be caught up in the crisis of God's purpose; through him and his preaching, the powers of the new age are made available to men, and his specific task is an aspect of what must come to pass in the course of the fulfilment of the divine plan. Frequently too it is affirmed that Paul's eschatological view placed his own work in the context of a series of fixed, known stages of eschatological expectation; within limits this is true, though Paul's adherence to a rigid eschatological scheme can easily be overemphasized.[5]

The function of the apostle appears with special clarity when Paul says that he is 'called to be an apostle, set apart for the gospel of God'.[6] Perhaps the term 'set apart' is a translation of

[1]'By his use of the term ['called'] St Paul places himself on a level at once with the great Old Testament saints and with the Twelve who had been "called" expressly by Christ' (Sanday and Headlam, p. 4; on Rom. 1.1).

[2]Gal. 1.15, cf. Jer. 1.5.

[3]II Cor. 3.18.

[4]II Cor. 3.1–11.

[5]Cf. O. Cullmann, *Christ and Time*, pp. 164–7; 'Le caractère eschatologique du devoir missionnaire . . .', *RHPR* XVI (1936), 210–45; 'Quand viendra le royaume de dieu?', *ibid.* XVIII (1938), 174–86; A. Fridrichsen, 'The Apostle and his message', *Uppsala Universitets Aarsskrift* (1947.3), 1–23; J. Munck, *Paul and the Salvation of Mankind* (ET), London, 1959. Noteworthy reviews of Munck's important book are those of W. D. Davies, *New Testament Studies* II (1955–6), 60–72, and Morton Smith, 'Pauline Problems', *HTR* L (1957), 107–32. Cf. also Munck's *Christus und Israel*, Copenhagen, 1956.

[6]Rom. 1.1.

the word from which 'Pharisee' ('separated one') is derived: the real 'Pharisee' is he who is 'set apart for the gospel of God'.[1] Similarly, in the same verse, 'called to be an apostle',[2] though not literally quoted from the Old Testament, reveals a conscious comparison with the great figures whom God had called in the past at critical turning points in his dealings with men: Abraham, Moses, and the prophets, as well, probably, as a comparison with his contemporaries, who had also been 'called' by Christ. Anton Fridrichsen holds that by designating himself a 'called apostle' (*klētos apostolos*), Paul means that he is 'a man who has been appointed to a proper place and a peculiar task in the series of events to be accomplished in the final days of this world'.[2] Fridrichsen has correctly identified the central thrust of Paul's self-understanding. God has called him to a task of immense dignity and significance, to be a representative of Christ through whom and through whose work the powers of the end of the age are made effective, and who thus actually carries forward the work of God toward its indescribable consummation.

The apostle, as that figure was conceived by Paul, was the bearer of the same message as the Church at large; he was set apart from the community by his special calling to represent Christ. Though the functions of administration and proclamation were never separated, in Paul's view the preaching function was primary, since it participated directly in the achievement of God's new purpose. The conflict between the two emphases was not simply the contrast between a 'missionary' and a 'bishop'. The tension between these two aspects of the work of an apostle is an instance of the tension between the conviction, on the one hand, that Christ is working through his chosen representative with a distinctive and uniquely new power, the power of the new age which was made available (although only to faith) through the resurrection of Christ, and, on the other hand, the necessary pre-occupation with the Church as a continuing social group subject to the same pressures as any group of human beings

[1] Schlatter, *Gottes Gerechtigkeit*, pp. 17 f.
[2] Rom. 1.1; I Cor. 1.1; but note that all believers are called in a different sense, i.e., 'called to be saints', Rom. 1.7; I Cor. 1.2; cf. Rom. 1.6; I Cor. 1.24. This, too, is an eschatological vocation.
[3] 'The Apostle and his message', p. 1.

working together in 'this world'. For the apostle's preaching was not merely eschatological in its subject matter; it was itself a part of the eschatological drama. The apostle was called, not just to build a group of believers, but to take part in the work of God which is to culminate in a wholly new order of existence.

This function of preaching is most clearly shown in Paul's discussion of the role of Israel in God's plan. In Rom. 11, the end cannot come 'until the full number of the Gentiles come in, and so all Israel shall be saved.'[1] This statement, the concluding point in an analysis of the meaning of Israel's rejection of Christ, affords a point of departure for a study of Paul's vocation as apostle. In Rom. 15 Paul writes,

> But on some points I have written to you very boldly by way of reminder, because of the grace given me by God to be a minister of Christ Jesus to the Gentiles in the priestly service of the gospel of God, so that the offering of the Gentiles may be acceptable, sanctified by the Holy Spirit. In Christ Jesus, then, I have reason to be proud of my work for God. For I will not venture to speak of anything except what Christ has wrought through me to win obedience from the Gentiles, by word and deed, by the power of signs and wonders, by the power of the Holy Spirit, so that from Jerusalem and as far round as Illyricum I have fully preached the gospel of Christ . . .[2]

Here Paul affirms that Christ works through him in the significant eschatological task of bringing in the full number of the Gentiles. Paul approached his work with the conviction that the time was short, and there is much truth in Munck's suggestion that he thought of 'the full number of the Gentiles' representatively; that is, each Gentile group or nation must have, collectively, the opportunity to repent and believe, and when this opportunity has been extended to all such groups, the restoration of Israel will occur, followed by the end.[3] This view would explain his haste to get on to Spain and thus, one might actually say, hasten the end.[4] Yet as so often with Paul, the formal eschatological pattern is transcended by his passionate eagerness to reach as many as possible, a passion which reflected his faith in the immeasurable,

[1]Rom. 11.25 f.
[2]Rom. 15.15–19.
[3]Munck, *op. cit.*, pp. 42–49.
[4]Rom. 15.23 f.

indescribable generosity of God's purpose.[1] But regardless of how closely one presses the formal eschatological scheme, the passage clearly indicates the dignity and importance which Paul attributed to his own work—or rather, Christ's work through him—Christ is completing the task of salvation begun in his own death and resurrection, and Paul has a uniquely significant task in that he is sent by Christ himself to the Gentiles; all his efforts are directed to a work which is a key phase of the very plan of God for history.[2]

Munck has urged the view that Paul understood the new opportunity of the Gentiles through a reversal of the Jewish Christian expectation that the transformation of the Jewish people into the new Israel of God would be followed by the conversion of the Gentiles. It is given to Paul to see that this seemingly logical pattern is actually to operate in reverse order: first the Gentiles will be saved, then the Jews.[3] This suggestion has much to commend it, particularly since it stresses Paul's concern for the salvation of both 'Jew and Greek', in contrast to the later Gentile Church which did not seriously concern itself with God's purpose for the Jews. Yet it must be received with caution, since the details of the eschatological pattern are often left unclear by Paul, and this lack of clarity results partly from his pressing beyond a formal scheme of eschatology to a perception of the character of God, as known in Christ, as the motivating force of his activity.

Oscar Cullmann, followed by Munck, has used the high sense of vocation of Paul to illuminate a well-known difficult passage in II Thess. 2. Paul is reminding the Thessalonians that the end cannot come at once, since there must be a terrible outburst of Satanic activity first. To this commonplace of apocalyptic thought he adds the following obscure note:

> And you know what is restraining him [the man of lawlessness] now so that he may be revealed in his time. For the mystery of lawlessness is already at work; only he who now restrains it will do so until he is out of the way. And then the lawless one will be revealed,

[1]I Cor. 9.19–23; cf. Rom. 11.33–36; see above, p. 50.
[2]Fridrichsen, *op. cit.,* p. 11.
[3]Munck, *op. cit.,* ch. 2. He finds the Pauline pattern of hope in Rom. 11, and the Jewish Christian pattern expressed in James' speech in Acts 15.15–18.

and the Lord Jesus will slay him with the breath of his mouth and destroy him by his appearing and coming.[1]

Something far clearer to the Thessalonians than to us is restraining the final outbreak of evil. Cullmann relates this passage to the eschatology of Rom. 11, and proposes the preaching of the gospel as the restraining factor which must come before the end.[2] 'What is restraining him' is the preaching of the gospel; 'he who now restrains it' is none other than Paul himself. Cullmann relates the idea of 'restraining' to Jewish discussions about what delays the end. One line of thought—the 'theocentric'—believed that the end is held back because God does not will for it to come; this line of thinking led to the attempt to forecast the date of the end from God's revelation, and was insufficient because though theocentric it was arbitrary. Another line of thought held that the end does not come because Israel fails to repent. This 'anthropocentric' view puts the responsibility for the failure of the end to come on human decision, and thus may be regarded as not treating the divine sovereignty seriously enough. None the less, Cullmann sees Paul's understanding of the role of the proclamation and of his own vocation as derived from such a pattern of thinking—modified by the stress on God's offer of the final, critical opportunity of repentance. Thus the emphasis is no longer on the human choice which delays the end but on the divine initiative which offers a final opportunity.

If Paul himself is 'he who restrains', then his death would be a key turning point in the pattern of God's purpose. Speaking of the restraining factor, Paul says, '. . . until he [who restrains] is out of the way. And then the lawless one will be revealed.'[3] Cullmann and Munck alike see this passage as confirming what Albert Schweitzer had affirmed earlier, in a different way—that Paul saw eschatological significance in his own death.[4]

---

[1]II Thess. 2.6–8.
[2]Cf. Mark 13.10.
[3]II Thess. 2.7 f.
[4]Schweitzer, in relating II Cor. 5.1–9 (which pictures an intermediate 'unclothed' state) to Phil. 1.21–24 (which expresses a hope of being immediately with Christ after death) holds that Paul believed in the intermediate state for Christians generally, but that his own self-consciousness of a special relationship to Christ made him think of himself as an exception. He hoped that a martyr's death would bring him, like Enoch and Elijah, a special resurrection. This view does not have any clear-cut evidence in its favour,

A broader view of Paul's self-understanding does not bear out the view that he saw eschatological significance in his own death. Rather, as he states it in Philippians, it is his life which had this significance:

> For to me to live is Christ, and to die is gain. If it is to be life in the flesh, that means fruitful labour for me . . . My desire is to depart and be with Christ, for that is far better. But to remain in the flesh is more necessary on your account.[1]

Here the high significance of death—to depart and be with Christ —is referred only to Paul's own individual self, and it will mark the termination of his participation in the active achievement of God's purpose as he understands it. Paul does not relate his death to the coming of the end. If this is so, then it is probably wrong to interpret II Thess. 2.6–8 as referring to Paul himself, though it is true that cosmic struggle and apostolic proclamation were conjoined by Paul. These verses probably refer to some aspect of cosmic struggle, and beyond that remain unclear to the modern reader.[2] But whether or not the particular reference of the obscure 'restrainer' of II Thessalonians is to Paul, the interpretation is significant in focusing attention on the way in which Paul saw connexions between concrete activity among men and the ultimate eschatological order.

Though Paul's understanding of his own death does not cast light on his thought about apostleship, there are many places in which he speaks of suffering as a necessary mark of his vocation. The apostle was the figure in whom the conflict between this present age and the age to come was most sharply set forth; as such he could only expect to bear the brunt of the opposition to Christ.[3] Consequently, suffering was a demonstration of the genu-

---

but Schweitzer is quite correct in observing, 'The challenge to his apostleship had had the effect of inflaming and intensifying his self-consciousness' (*The Mysticism of Paul the Apostle*, trans. William Montgomery, London, 1931, pp. 135–7).

[1]Phil. 1.21–24.
[2]J. Christiaan Beker accepts Munck's view of II Thess. 2.6–8 but regards this exegesis as evidence that Paul did not write II Thessalonians; i.e., he fails to find support in Paul's thought generally for such an interpretation of his death. Cf. his review of Charles Masson's *Thessaloniciens* (CNT 11a: 1957) in the *Journal of Religion* XXXVIII (1958), 131–2.
[3]I Cor. 4.9–13; II Cor. 6.3–10.

ineness of his apostleship as against the view (apparently held by his detractors at Corinth) that the honour of appointment by God meant success and pre-eminence.[1] But though Paul does point to his hardships as signs of the reality of his calling and his message, and though he ironically contrasts his hard lot with the ease of the Corinthians, the suffering of the apostle is not a contrast to, but a paradigm for the community as a whole. Just as all are called to proclaim the gospel, so all are called to suffer.[2]

The intensity of Paul's sense of vocation has led some students to conclude that he held that there were very few apostles called as he was. Thus Fridrichsen affirms, 'In this world, soon disappearing, the centre is Jerusalem with the primitive community and the Twelve, surrounded by the mission-field divided between two apostles: one sent by the Lord to the circumcised, the other to the Gentiles.'[3]

A principal support for this view is found in Galatians:

. . . When they saw that I had been entrusted with the gospel to the uncircumcised, just as Peter had been entrusted with the gospel to the circumcised (for he who worked through Peter for the mission to the circumcised worked through me also for the Gentiles), and when they perceived the grace that was given to me, James and Cephas and John, who were reputed to be pillars, gave to me and Barnabas the right hand of fellowship, that we should go to the Gentiles, and they to the circumcised . . . [4]

There are other passages where Paul asserts his high or nearly-unique position: he 'worked harder than any of them'.[5] When the references to a special position for Paul are read in the setting of eschatological expectation which required the proclamation of the gospel to the whole world, and in connexion with Paul's vivid sense of *his own* importance and *his* gospel's importance, it is easy to conclude that Paul viewed himself as uniquely chosen by God to be a kind of prophetic forerunner of the end.[6]

[1] II Cor. 11.23–33. Cf. E. Käsemann, 'Die Legitimität des Apostels', *Zeitschrift für die neutestamentliche Wissenschaft* XLI (1942), 53–56; Munck, *op. cit.*, pp. 186 f.
[2] See below, pp. 111–15.
[3] *Op. cit.*, p. 6. Similarly John Knox, 'A note on the text of Romans', *New Testament Studies* II (1955–6), 191.
[4] Gal. 2.7–9.
[5] I Cor. 15.10.
[6] Cf. Munck, *op. cit.*, p. 41.

The merits of such a view must not be judged by its correspondence to the use of the term 'apostle'. For Paul does not limit this term to a small, easily definable group. To him all apostles are representatives of Christ. This is the meaning, whether or not he adds the phrase 'of Christ'.[1] All apostles were empowered by Christ to proclaim the gospel,[2] and thus all participate in the eschatological task. It has been suggested that in early Christian usage these representatives called apostles were divided into two classes: 'apostles' of Christ in the strict sense, and 'missionaries', the latter commissioned by churches rather than by Christ. But this distinction appears to rest on a later conception that there were only twelve apostles. Paul himself never distinguishes the two types.[3] As to the method of appointment there might be a variation. For Paul the term 'apostle' as a technical term means 'apostle of Christ'.[4]

As Paul describes them, the specific functions of apostles included preaching and founding churches, and itinerancy was a common feature of their activity.[5] The powers of the new age in the apostle are reflected in the miraculous signs which Paul mentions but does not emphasize.[6] No one feature can be claimed as a necessary mark of the apostle, however; there was probably a good deal of fluidity in their actual activities.[7] In other words,

[1] I Cor. 1.1; II Cor. 1.1; Col. 1.1; cf. Gal. 1.1.

[2] This is a clear implication of I Cor. 15.9–11, where Paul compares his achievements with those of the other apostles. Cf. also Rom. 16.7, where Andronicus and Junias, notable apostles, have been imprisoned, presumably as Christian missionaries; I Cor. 9.5, where the phrase 'be accompanied by a wife' suggests missionary activity; I Cor. 4.9; 12.28, which show the familiarity of the Corinthians with the office, and the clearly missionary activity of the 'superlative apostles' or 'false apostles' of II Cor. 11.5, 13; 12.11.

[3] Note, however, Gal. 1.1, where Paul calls himself 'an apostle—not from men nor through man, but through Jesus Christ and God the Father'. Burton maintains that this passage indicates that Paul knew of apostles who received their commission from men, that is, from the Jerusalem apostles. Cf. E. de W. Burton, *Galatians* (ICC), Edinburgh, 1921, pp. 3, 377 f.

[4] *Ibid.*, pp. 364 f.

[5] I Cor. 9.2, 5.

[6] II Cor. 12.12; Rom. 15.19.

[7] If James was regarded as an apostle (the apparent meaning of Gal 1.19), travelling and founding churches can probably not be regarded as essential qualifications of an apostle. Free support was given others besides apostles (I Cor. 9.5), and miraculous activity was expected to be present in all proclamation of the gospel (cf. I Cor. 2.4). Cf. von Campenhausen, *Studia Theologica* I, 111.

it was not any specific activity which marked the apostle, but rather his authoritative 'direct' representation of Christ.

The apostle's commission to represent Christ was apparently in all cases associated with a meeting with the risen Christ.[1] Yet one cannot absolutely insist that this was the only fashion in which such a vocation was given, since the evidence that Paul linked apostleship with a resurrection appearance is not so unambiguous as is frequently supposed.[2] Vocation by the Lord mediated by the community as his representatives may have been recognized by others in Early Christianity, but not by Paul. No doubt churches did appoint delegates and missionaries,[3] but these are nowhere approximated to apostles of Christ by Paul. He never mentions his own appointment by any church; in fact, he strongly rejects the suggestion that he acquired his apostleship in any such way.[4]

Thus Paul recognizes a fairly definite and limited group of apostles, but makes clear that who precisely belonged to the group could become a matter of vigorous debate. Apostles at Paul's time were not the 'twelve' but a larger group. Paul refers to the twelve only once, and then clearly distinguishes them from the apostles as a whole.[5] Not all witnesses to the resurrection, on the other hand, were apostles.[6] It has been maintained that in distinguishing between 'the twelve' and 'the apostles' Paul meant, by the apostles, 'the twelve plus James'.[7] But it is difficult to limit the term in this way, both because it would be peculiar to

---

[1]In I Cor. 15.7, 'all the apostles' witness the resurrection; in I Cor. 9.1, 'apostle' and 'seeing the Lord' are joined. In Gal. 1.15–16, 'revealing his son to me' is coupled to the 'preaching among the nations'.

[2]Lake, *Beginnings* V, pp. 50 f.; von Campenhausen, *op. cit.*, pp. 113 f.

[3]Called *apostoloi*, II Cor. 8.23, Phil. 2.25.

[4]Gal. 1.1.

[5]I Cor. 15.5, 7.

[6]I Cor. 15.6. W. G. Kümmel, *Kirchenbegriff und Geschichtsbewusstsein in der Urgemeinde und bei Jesus* (Symbolae Biblicae Upsalienses I), 1943, pp. 4 f., holds that only the phrase, 'that he appeared to Cephas then to the twelve', is to be taken as the old tradition which Paul quotes. The rest of the list is to be taken as Paul's own formulation on the basis of current tradition. Even so, the list demonstrates that there was a recognized distinction between 'apostles' and 'the twelve' on the one hand, and 'apostles' and 'witnesses to the resurrection' on the other.

[7]K. Holl, 'Der Kirchenbegriff des Paulus . . .', *Gesammelte Aufsätze zur Kirchengeschichte*, Tübingen, 1928, II, pp. 48 f.

have two technical terms for groups so nearly identical, and because Paul uses the word apostle in other places, apparently as a current term, in a sense which clearly includes others.[1]

Even more suggestive than Paul's casual references to other apostles is the fact that he had to contend with men whom he could not recognize as apostles, yet who apparently claimed a station as exalted as his own. The 'superlative apostles' of II Corinthians are not the leaders at Jerusalem, for Paul could not have described them as 'false apostles'.[2] Whoever these 'apostles beyond measure' were, their conflict with Paul shows the 'open' character of the apostolic group, while at the same time Paul's sarcastic denunciation of them may indicate that they, like himself, claimed some special recognition among the apostles.

Paul neither narrowly restricts the group of apostles, nor distinguishes within it between apostles of Christ and apostles of the churches, yet his writings none the less show that he understood himself as having a special vocation among the apostles. Though he never speaks of himself as 'the apostle to the gentiles', he does hold that God had chosen him for a special place within the task of proclamation.[3] In some sense he believed that he was the most significant apostle. Even though we reject the view that Paul saw special importance in his own death in relation to the divine purpose, and likewise note his application of the term 'apostle' to a wider group, others of whom beside himself worked among the Gentiles, it remains evident that Paul held that he was in a special way important in the apostolic group.

[1]Andronicus and Junias, Rom. 16.7 (though it is possible to take the Greek as meaning 'noteworthy to the apostles'); Barnabas, I Cor. 9.4–6; probably James, Gal. 1.19; possibly Silvanus, I Thess. 2.6. However the definite limits of the term are clearly shown by the fact that he carefully refrains from calling Timothy an apostle (e.g., II Cor. 1.1).

[2]II Cor. 11.5, 13–15; 12.11; Lietzmann, *An die Korinther, ad. loc.*; Kümmel, *Kirchenbegriff*, p. 6; Munck, *op. cit.*, pp. 177 f.; see J. Héring, *II Corinthiens, ad. loc.*, for the opposite view.

[3]In Rom. 11.13, Paul speaks of himself as 'an apostle' to the Gentiles, according to the usage of the Greek definite article with predicate nouns. See E. C. Colwell, 'A definite rule for the use of the article in the Greek New Testament', *JBL* LII (1933), 12–21. The absence of an article is not conclusive here since there is a tendency to omit it with predicate nouns, yet its addition would have been required had Paul wished to emphasize that he was *the* apostle to the Gentiles (see Blass-Debrunner, *Grammatik des neutestamentlichen Griechisch*, 9th ed., Göttingen, 1954, § 273). The context would make

The unique role of Paul is rightly connected with his vision of
the place of the Gentiles in the gracious purpose of God.[1] That
Paul's immense conviction of his own importance in the unfolding
cosmic drama was connected with a new insight into the order of
eschatological events is probable. He held that the Gentiles would
be saved before Jews. Yet this form of structure of 'fixed events'
is only the vehicle through which Paul becomes aware of the
indescribable goodness of God in Christ, and the deeper awareness
of God's goodness makes itself known both in the transformation
of the formal pattern of 'representative collective proclamation'
into an intense concern to reach all if possible, and in the openness with which he acknowledges that others are called into the
same task as he is. Here there is a kind of paradox in Paul's
vocation, for the very awareness of the divine presence which
raises him to a height of self-awareness also makes him understand that this same dignity and honour may be conferred on
others, and indeed are, though in less marked degree, conferred
on the whole Church which functions as a whole in God's
eschatological purpose just as Paul does.

When the challenge to his authority made it necessary for him
to affirm his rightful position, he boldly claimed to be the one
who could set the standard for the right understanding of the
gospel, whether against those who imperfectly saw the newness
of the eschatological situation with its demand of faith, or against
those who held that their own inner awareness of the Spirit
relieved them of the responsibility of responsible participation
in the community. Paul's vigorous assertion of his apostolic
authority is significant not only because it drives him to give a
'phenomenological description of the true apostolate',[2] but more
importantly because it was a factor in establishing the later,
predominantly authoritative conception of what an apostle was.
As the sense of eschatological participation weakened, the high
authority of the apostle was what the Church saw in Paul's interpretation of himself.

this a most appropriate place for Paul to claim to be 'the apostle to the
Gentiles' had he wished to do so.

[1]Fridrichsen, *op. cit., passim*; Munck, *op. cit.*, pp. 45–9.
[2]J. Héring, *II Corinthiens*, p. 83.

Apart from this power-struggle—except in so far as it provides the occasion for his self-disclosure—it is evident that his calling as apostle provides Paul's highest form of understanding how God may work through a chosen man. The apostle is called by God (or Christ) and takes part in the work of God. His activity is to find its ultimate significance and completion in the new order, and his proclamation of the gospel plays a part in the series of events which in the divine purpose 'must' take place. Yet the apostle works in a concrete and indeed growing community in which the patterns of the present age must be either rejected or transformed. The apostle's position in this community is unique not only in his position of authority but because of his conscious understanding of his place in the divine plan. Thus as apostle Paul shows his conviction, similar to that of the prophets, that human personality is not simply passive in the hands of God, but that it may, through God's initiating choice, become an active and conscious element even in happenings of cosmic significance.

VI

SLAVE AND SERVANT OF GOD; PROPHET AND MARTYR

SLAVE

In Paul's writings the word *doulos* means 'slave', rather than 'servant', as it is usually translated. The force of Paul's use of slavery as a metaphor has been largely lost, for the English reader, by the use of the vaguer term 'servant'. Of the well-known English versions, only Goodspeed consistently translates 'slave'. Moffatt retains 'servant' throughout. The RSV has introduced 'slave' for some of Paul's usages, but where he speaks of the *doulos* of Christ or of the Church, it keeps 'servant'.[1]

Subjection was the meaning of slavery, both to Paul and to his readers.[2] Therefore it is not surprising to find slavery appearing as a metaphor for the subjection in which Paul believed men to be apart from Christ. This subjection is seen by Paul in a cosmic framework. The creation itself is not what God intended it to be, and exists, like men, in a state of 'slavery to corruption' and of agonized expectation of its deliverance.[3] The cosmic powers appear as themselves unfriendly when Paul speaks of slavery to 'the elemental spirits of the universe'.[4] Worshippers of pagan gods are subject to the cosmic powers, and Paul seems to have regarded pagan deities as real manifestations of cosmic or

[1] In this chapter *doulos* ('slave') and *diakonos* ('servant') and related terms are frequently translated literally instead of following the usage of the RSV.

[2] K. H. Rengstorf, '*doulos*', *TWNT*, II, 273.

[3] Rom. 8.19–23; cf. Sanday and Headlam, p. 207; Lietzmann, *An die Römer*, pp. 84 f. It is possible to understand 'the creation' in this passage as 'mankind', rather than the whole creation; then the contrast is between the redeemed and the rest of mankind. Cf. Schlatter, *op. cit.*, p. 273; Emil Brunner, *Revelation and Reason*, trans. Olive Wyon, London, 1947, p. 72. The analogies in Jewish apocalyptic make it more probable that Paul is here speaking of a cosmic slavery; cf. II (4) Esdras 7.11–12. However, Schlatter's interpretation of 'the creation' is significant as a reminder that Paul's conception of God's purpose is firmly centred on the relationship between God and men.

[4] Gal. 4.3, 9; cf. Col. 2.20.

demonic forces, in spite of the fact that such pagan gods are 'by nature no gods',[1] and are called, in the language of Jewish apologetic, 'idols'.[2] But Judaism too is caught in the same bondage. In particular, the law is a manifestation of a compulsive, sub-personal, cosmic power, and those who reverence it will become enslaved once more by the elemental spirits of the universe.[3] Thus the cosmic powers are real forces against which Christ had to struggle, and from which freedom can be found only in Christ.[4]

The powers which enslave man are, however, significant because they enter into man's moral life. The cosmic setting of the moral struggle does not interest Paul for its own sake—a point in which he stands in marked contrast to many speculative writers of both apocalyptic and gnostic schools. Various terms describe the slavery in which man finds himself, from the point of view of its impact on man's character. Some men are slaves of 'their own appetites', which is to say that their appetite is 'their god'.[5] By ignoring the meaning of what Christ has done, one may become a slave 'of men', i.e., of the opinions commonly held by men.[6] And in actual practice freedom from the 'elemental spirits' means freedom from 'human precepts and doctrines'.[7] Likewise the churches are subject to the danger of being enslaved by men, i.e., of giving their allegiance to a human leader instead of to Christ.[8] But the most general description of human bondage is

---

[1]Gal. 4.8; cf. I Cor. 8.4–6.

[2]I Thess. 1.9.

[3]Gal. 4.3–4. Cf. H. Lietzmann, *An die Galater* (HNT 10), 2nd ed., Tübingen, 1923, p. 24.

[4]I Cor. 2.8; Col. 1.13; 2.15. The above discussion assumes that the *stoicheia* of Gal. 4.3, 9; Col. 2.8, 20 are cosmic powers; cf. Lietzmann, *An die Galater*, pp. 24 f.; Pierre Bonnard, *Galates* (CNT 9), Paris, 1952, pp. 84–5. Even if, with Burton, *Galatians*, p. 518, this term is taken to mean 'elementary and imperfect teachings of religion', the main point made above is validated from other Pauline passages, esp. I Cor. 2.6, 8.

[5]Rom. 16.18; Phil. 3.19.

[6]I Cor. 7.23.

[7]Col. 2.22.

[8]II Cor. 11.20; Gal. 2.4. Paul recognized that loyalty to him could constitute such a slavery (I Cor. 1.10–17), but cf. the comments of J. Knox (*Chapters in a Life of Paul*, London, 1954, p. 96), who sees a tension between the desire that loyalty to Christ should come before any partisan loyalty, and an intense desire for the love and loyalty of his own churches.

slavery to sin.¹ Here again, sin appears as an overmastering power, which not even the law can overcome. The double aspect of 'slavery' is shown by the fact that the power of sin is both something inescapable, and the fruit of consent.² Correspondingly, the moral struggle is described as a kind of dual allegiance.³ It is to be observed that slavery does not suggest mere passive submission; it is an active, not a static metaphor:

> Do you not know that if you yield yourselves to any one as obedient slaves, you are slaves of the one whom you obey, either of sin, which leads to death, or of obedience, which leads to righteousness?⁴

Slavery means participation in a process; the ends are determined by that to which one is enslaved. As usual, it is as a process, rather than as a status, that Paul views man's life.

The contrast between slavery and freedom was a familiar one in the Hellenistic world, and Deissmann has well emphasized the force of the pictorial description of the 'glorious liberty of the sons of God'.⁵ Significant for the understanding of Paul's thought, however, is the fact that he can with equal ease speak of the new life as a new kind of slavery. In accordance with the principle, 'If you yield yourselves to any one as obedient slaves, you are slaves of the one you obey,'⁶ it is clear that for Paul human life must be lived in subjection to a higher power. There is no such thing as autonomy, for him, and the freedom of which he speaks is a quite different thing from the freedom of the Stoics.⁷ Freedom consists in obedience; in fact, the new life can

¹Rom. 6–7.
²Rom. 7.5–6; 6.12–19.
³Rom. 7.25b; cf. Matt. 6.24.
⁴Rom. 6.16.
⁵Adolf Deissmann, *Light from the Ancient East* (ET), new ed., London, 1927, pp. 318–25, suggested that sacral manumission provided the key to much of Paul's use of the metaphors of slavery and freedom. Rengstorf, '*doulos*', 278 n. 106, holds that the purely fictitious nature of this transaction makes the analogy too remote, and holds that the only significant parallel in Hellenistic culture was the simple transfer of ownership of a slave. F. Solokowski, 'The real meaning of sacral manumission', *HTR* XLVII (1954), 173–81, develops further legal details of manumission and holds that this special procedure supplies much of the Pauline imagery.
⁶Rom. 6.16.
⁷Slavery is often used by Epictetus as a symbol of that rule of the passions or of external things from which the wise man must deliver himself (Epict.,

be described as 'slavery to obedience',[1] as well as slavery to righteousness,[2] or to God,[3] or to Christ.[4] This sort of language is quite foreign to the Greek world, where *doulos* was almost unknown as a religious term and where slavery was too 'servile' to be thought an appropriate religious metaphor.[5] In Oriental religions and in the Old Testament, however, the idea that the worshipper was a slave of the deity was common.[6] There are analogies in the Greek world to Paul's contrast of slavery with freedom. But the description of the religious life as a kind of slavery, rather than as a kind of freedom, was something Eastern rather than Greek, and in Paul distinctively Hebraic. The parallels in the mystery religions are remote, as they relate the 'slavery to the god' to a formal act of initiation, while in Paul the metaphor springs from his conception of the dynamics of obedience.[7] The ease with which Paul thinks of slavery to God or to Christ, and the facility with which he slips from the metaphor of freedom to that of a new slavery,[8] find their background in the Hebrew and Jewish conception of the relationship between God and men. The specific origin of the slavery terminology is the Septuagint. There the people as a whole are called 'slaves of God',[9] and the individual worshipper may be a 'slave of God',[10] so that 'to serve' comes to mean simply 'worship'.[11] The change that Paul makes is that Christ, rather than God, is usually the 'master'; just as the Old Testament epithet 'Lord' is regularly applied to Christ by Paul.[12]

Diss. iii.22, 40, 42; 24, 67). Though the free man is spoken of as a servant (Epict., *Diss.* iii.26.28; iii.24.98) of god, his freedom is his own achievement, and consists in detaching himself from the things not under his control (*ibid.*, iv.1 *passim*).

[1] Rom. 6.16.
[2] Rom. 6.18.
[3] Rom. 6.22; cf. Rom. 7.6; in I Thess. 1.9, 'to serve' has its LXX sense, 'worship'.
[4] I Cor. 7.22; cf. Eph. 6.6. In Rom. 12.11; 14.18; the meaning 'slavery' predominates as against the meaning 'worship'.
[5] H. J. Rose, *Ancient Greek Religion*, London, 1946, p. 12.
[6] Rengstorf, *'doulos'*, 268–72.
[7] *Ibid.*, 271 f., 278.
[8] As in Rom. 6–7.
[9] Isa. 63.17; cf. 48.20.
[10] Ps. 27.9 (26.9); 31.16 (30.17); cf. Lietzmann, *An die Römer*, pp. 22 f.
[11] Judg. 10.16 (MS B), etc.
[12] See below, pp. 120 f.

The value of the service rendered by the slave is usually secondary, as Paul uses the metaphor. The element of service does appear, however, when he speaks of himself, or of Christians generally, as slaves of the community as a whole or of one another.[1] Even here, however, the element of submission is prominent. Paul's 'slavery to other men' consists in his accommodating himself to their point of view, and the servitude of Christians to one another is a slavery of humble love.[2] Likewise the description of Christ as a slave suggests humility and service, and these are expressed in obedience.[3] Thus for Paul the total submission of slavery is not too strong a comparison for the obedience due to God, and in this broadly metaphorical sense it provides a way of describing the situation of all believers.

Slavery to Christ also appears in Paul's writings in a special sense. The word 'slave' is used as a specific title by which Paul describes his own calling and that of the Christian leader. He calls himself a 'slave of Christ'; therefore he is not answerable to men.[4] He describes himself alone,[5] and in conjunction with Timothy,[6] by this title. Epaphras is also named a 'slave of Christ Jesus',[7] while he and Tychicus are affectionately called 'fellow slaves'.[8] The same idea of special relationship to a master is present, though obscured in the translation, when Paul describes his missionary activity as being led in triumph by God in Christ.[9] The picture is that of a slave in the victor's triumphal procession; Paul is saying that he is only a slave, but that his activity is part of a triumphal procession—that of God.[10] Thus even when 'slave' appears as an 'honorific' of the Christian leader, an important element in its meaning is the affirmation that the leader himself is nothing; it is God's (or, usually, Christ's) activity in and through him that

[1] I Cor. 9.19; II Cor. 4.5; Gal. 5.13.
[2] Gal. 5.13; cf. Phil. 2.3.
[3] Phil. 2.7.
[4] Gal. 1.10.
[5] Rom. 1.1.
[6] Phil. 1.1; 2.22; thus the title may be applied to his assistants; though the term 'apostle' is not applied to them.
[7] Col. 4.12.
[8] Col. 1.7; 4.7.
[9] II Cor. 2.14.
[10] G. Delling, '*thriambeuō*', *TWNT*, III, 159–60; Plummer, *II Corinthians*, p. 68.

gives him his significance. Though he acts and chooses, his Master directs him; he belongs to God.[1]

Like the general use of 'slave' for the worshipper, this special use has its background in the Septuagint. A specially chosen instrument of Yahweh may be called a 'slave of God'. Moses and David are so named, as are others.[2] The term becomes almost a technical designation for the prophets, usually in a context which specifically indicates that they are instruments of God's action.[3] In this Septuagint title the element of submission is indeed presupposed, but the emphasis lies on the point that the action of the 'slave' is really God's—in this person God is at work.[4]

Such a conception of the slave of God stands behind Paul's choice of the term to describe himself and other eminent leaders of the Church. Dependence and obedience must characterize them, as it must all who are in Christ. But the leaders are 'slaves of Christ' in a special sense, because they have been chosen by Christ to have a part in the work which he is accomplishing.[5] Sanday and Headlam observe:

> . . . it is noticeable how quietly St Paul steps into the place of the prophets and leaders of the Old Covenant, and how quietly he substitutes the name of his own Master in a connection hitherto reserved for that of Jehovah.[6]

The most distinctive feature of Paul's language is the substitution, in this borrowed Old Testament phrase, of the name of Christ for that of God. This change reflects not only the vividness of Paul's personal attachment to Christ, but also his conviction that he was specially called to take part in the work of Christ. Paul's phrase, 'slave of Christ', occurs elsewhere in the New Testament, but not extensively.[7] It was soon replaced by the old

---

[1] Rengstorf, '*doulos*', 280. In all the variety of Paul's use of the slavery metaphor, man appears as 'the master' only once, when Paul speaks of 'subduing' his body, I Cor. 9.27.

[2] II Kings 18.12; II Sam. 7.5; I Macc. 4.30; II Macc. 1.2; cf. Lietzmann, *An die Römer*, pp. 22 f.

[3] Amos 3.7; cf. Jer. 7.25; Dan. 9.6 (Theodotion).

[4] G. Sass, 'Zur Bedeutung von *doulos* bei Paulus', *Zeitschrift für die neutestamentliche Wissenschaft* XL (1941), 26.

[5] *Ibid.*, 30–2; Lietzmann, *An die Römer*, p. 23.

[6] Sanday and Headlam, p. 3.

[7] James 1.1; II Peter 1.1; Jude 1.

term 'slave of God'.[1] This change, too, is a witness to the special meaning which the expression had for Paul. The 'slave of Christ' was the specially chosen agent through whom Christ carried on his work, and prepared for its great consummation. As the Church ceased to think in terms of the establishment by God, or Christ, of a new era, it adopted a more general terminology. Thus though Paul does not apply to himself, or to other leaders of the Church, the term 'prophet' in its Old Testament meaning, he borrows from the Greek Bible a term expressing a 'prophetic' sense of vocation.

SERVANT

A term closely related to 'slave' is *diakonos,* 'servant'. Commonly the word was used to mean a personal servant,[2] and it had a specific meaning as 'waiter'.[3] Hence the word usually implied work of a menial nature, and when used as an adjective meant simply 'menial'.[4] On the other hand, the word focused attention on the work done rather than on the relationship to the person served. To be a 'servant' signified to work for some one, either in the sense of doing work commanded by him, or in the sense of doing work which helped him. Thus unlike 'slave', which because of its strong implication of subjection never became a religious term in Greek thought, 'servant' is freely used as a religious term by Hellenistic writers, and appears to come to Paul from Hellenistic usage, as 'slave' comes from Semitic.[5]

In the early Church the word *diakonos* is best known as the title of a church officer, the 'deacon'. Probably this title was derived from the usage of *diakonos* in Greek civic and religious organizations as the title of a minor official, though the exact function of such officials is not well known.[6] It appears that the original functions of the Christian *diakonoi* were administrative, though it

---

[1]Titus 1.1, modelled on the LXX.
[2]Herod., *Hist.* 4.71, 72; 9.82.
[3]Philo, *De Vita Contemplativa* 10.75; cf. John 2.5.
[4]Liddell and Scott, *s.v.*
[5]*Diakonos* is rare in the LXX. It means the royal eunuchs in Esth. 1.10; 2.2; (6.1, 3, 5, rdg.); 'servant' in Prov. 10.4; the agents of Antiochus in IV Macc. 9.17. Thus the LXX offers no basis for its religious usage.
[6]Moulton and Milligan, *op. cit.*, p. 149; H. Lietzmann, 'Zur altchristliche Verfassungsgeschichte', *Zeitschrift für wissenschaftliche Theologie* LV (1913–14), 108, 111–13.

has been held that their function was primarily liturgical from the start.[1] In any case, it is clear that Paul's understanding of what it means to be a servant of God or of Christ is not related to this official use, whether in ancient civic and religious groups or in the Church.

There is, however, in addition to the general idea of service, another possible avenue to the understanding of how a word implying menial service came to be used as a term for the servant of God. In classical Greek the word may mean 'messenger'.[2] The term is given as an equivalent for 'ambassador' by a grammarian of the second century AD.[3] It is possible that the two terms are associated in order to indicate that the ambassador is not an independent agent but is limited by the instructions given by his sender. Stephanus suggested that the meaning 'ambassador' lies behind Paul's use of the phrase 'servant of God'.[4] It is not unlikely that this same association lies behind its general religious use; it signifies representation as well as service, as in Epictetus and Philo.[5]

In Paul's writings, the two terms *doulos* and *diakonos* are parallel, and there is no doubt that subjection and obedience are implied in *diakonos*. Yet the different emphasis of the term is apparent in the fact that *diakonos*, in none of its uses, explicitly emphasizes subjection, as *doulos* often does. Even where Christ is spoken of as a *diakonos*, the passages fix attention on the action and its results, not on the subjection or humiliation which it involved.[6] The 'servant', unlike the 'slave', can be thought of with apparent indifference as the servant of God or of Christ—evidence that the word 'servant' does not signify a personal relationship so much

[1]Lietzmann, 'Altchristliche Verfassungsgeschichte', p. 109; F. J. A. Hort, *The Christian Ecclesia*, London, 1897, pp. 198–202. Dix (in *The Apostolic Ministry*, pp. 244–6) sees the diaconate arising from the specialization of a liturgical function; Manson, *The Church's Ministry*, pp. 60–5, emphasizes the fluidity of administrative arrangements at Paul's period.

[2]Aesch., *Prom. Vinc.* 942; Soph., *Philoc.* 497; *Frag.* 133, cited in Liddell and Scott, *s.v.*

[3]Julius Pollux, *Onomasticon* viii.11.137.

[4]H. Stephanus, *Thesaurus Graecae linguae* (new ed.; London, 1816–28), vol. IV, col. 5202.

[5]Epict., *Diss.* iii.22.69, 70; 26.28; Philo, *De Gig.* 3.12; *De Joseph.* 40.241.

[6]'Christ became a servant to the circumcised to show God's truthfulness, in order to confirm the promises given to the patriarchs,' Rom. 15.8; '. . . if . . . we ourselves were found to be sinners, is Christ then an agent of sin? Certainly not!' Gal. 2.17. Note the contrast with Christ as *doulos*, Phil. 2.7.

as a commission to work. This is also indicated by the fact that the 'servant' is often qualified according to his particular task. Paul describes himself as a minister or servant of 'a new covenant',[1] and of 'the gospel'.[2]

Active participation in a task, working for a cause, is also the significance of *diakonia,* which describes his work for the gospel of Christ. Being apostle to the Gentiles is his task, which is a *diakonia* of reconciliation.[3] Paul's consciousness of the significance of this task in the divine economy can be seen in his comparison of his *diakonia* with that of Moses. In comparison to the new service guided and given life by the Spirit, that of Moses was a 'service of condemnation'.[4] By implication Paul raises himself even above Moses, in respect of the part he plays in God's economy; and this understanding of his role is the basis on which he can be 'very bold'.[5] The service is that of an intermediary; the real power at work is Christ, so that the results are Christ's work. 'You are a letter from Christ delivered by us.'[6]

Thus the service of the servant of God appears in Paul's writings as obedient representation of God. This conception in itself is nothing new. Philo, Epictetus and others use it. What is new is the conception of God and of God's eschatological purpose, and the resulting conception of the task which is given. Paul associates this Hellenistic term integrally with the new work which he finds God doing in Christ, so that the 'service' becomes on the one hand a vigorous personal dedication,[7] and on the other, the participation in a new era, far exceeding in glory and permanence that of Moses.[8]

A related word, also used incidentally by Paul to describe his work, is *leitourgos* ('servant') which originally signified primarily the rendering of service to the state. In later times it came to have a much broader meaning, often being equivalent to 'worker'.[9]

[1]II Cor. 3.6.
[2]Col. 1.23; cf. Eph. 3.7.
[3]Rom. 11.13; II Cor. 5.18.
[4]II Cor. 3.7–11; see above, p. 83.
[5]II Cor. 3.12; cf. Plummer, *II Corinthians*, p. 91; Menzies, *op. cit.*, p. 23.
[6]II Cor. 3.3.
[7]II Cor. 6.3–10.
[8]II Cor. 3.7–11.
[9]Moulton and Milligan, *op. cit.*, p. 373.

In the Septuagint it is used for service to God, and specifically for the service of priests.[1] Paul uses this word in its general sense.[2] But when he speaks of himself as a *leitourgos*, the metaphor is the priestly one: Paul is the priest who consecrates the offering of the Gentiles.[3] In this passage, as elsewhere, Paul emphasizes the direct divine commission which he has received, and the consequent boldness and freedom of action which he exercised. The comparison of himself to a priest suggests his being set apart for a divinely-appointed task.

It has been noted above that one of the connotations of *diakonos* may be 'ambassador'.[4] Paul explicitly describes himself as an ambassador: 'So we are ambassadors for Christ, God making his appeal through us.'[5] His work as an ambassador is precisely the 'ministry of reconciliation'.[6]

The very clear similarity of the 'servant' terminology between Paul and the Stoics reflects certain similarities of thought. Both regarded their work as the strenuous, wholehearted, disciplined service of a reality greater than themselves. But, for the Stoics, this reality was a fact to be accepted, while for Paul it was an active will which determined the changing course of all existence, directing it to a goal, and which also determined his own existence, even giving him a part in the work by which the situation of men was being changed.[7]

This study of the meaning of 'slave', 'servant' and related terms has shown the fluidity of Paul's vocabulary. 'Servant' and 'ambassador' are metaphors rather than technical terms; 'slave'

[1]Sanday and Headlam, p. 405.
[2]Rom. 13.6; Phil. 2.25.
[3]Rom. 15.15–16.
[4]See above, p. 102
[5]II Cor. 5.20, using the verb; cf. Eph. 6.20.
[6]II Cor. 5.18. The noun 'ambassador', does not occur unless the conjectural emendation *presbeutēs* ('ambassador') for *presbytēs* ('old man') is accepted in Philemon 9; cf. Knox, *Chapters*, p. 74, who favours the emendation, and Lightfoot, *Colossians and Philemon*, pp. 336 f., who accepts the meaning 'ambassador' without a change in orthography. Deissmann, *op. cit.*, p. 374, notes that in the Greek East 'ambassador' was a technical term for the Emperor's legate, and notes that the verb 'to be entrusted' (I Cor. 9.17; Gal. 2.7) was also used in connexion with Imperial officials.
[7]The relation between Pauline and Stoic vocation has been well presented by K. Deissner, 'Das Sendungsbewusstsein der Urchristenheit', *Zeitschrift für systematische Theologie* VII (1929–30), 772–90.

is also metaphorical rather than technical in some of its uses. Only 'slave of Christ' becomes a technical term. Paul's language is drawn both from Judaism and Hellenism, as the parallel use of 'slave' and 'servant' makes clear. In all these metaphors, whatever their source, the same conception of man's significance appears: that a man, himself unable to work any lasting achievement, may be chosen by God, and lifted into the highest personal significance by being given a part in God's task. Thus the terms discussed in this chapter disclose, in more flexible language, the same conception of vocation which is to be seen in the term 'apostle'. Hence the study of 'slave' and 'servant' has confirmed the view of Paul's understanding of his task developed in the study of apostle. All these terms in common suggest that Paul's work is not undertaken and carried out on his own initiative, but that he has been 'laid hold on', not merely as a member of the body of Christ, but as the recipient of a special task. This conviction represents a sharpening of Paul's general view that all Christians have been given tasks not 'according to their abilities' but by the Spirit, 'who apportions to each one individually as he wills'.[1]

These terms also suggest that in Paul's work God, through Christ, is at work. In encountering Paul's activity one encounters the work of Christ. Thus there is nothing 'servile' about the slave of Christ. He is nothing, yet his commission gives him dignity and authority. His choices and his labours are expressions of the will of Christ; in them Christ is present.

PROPHET

In contrast to 'slave' and 'servant', two other terms are to be noted briefly, which in other writings are used to bear the meaning of prophetic vocation, but are not so used by Paul. These are 'prophet' and 'martyr'.

Our knowledge of prophecy in Paul's thought and in the life of his churches comes largely from the Corinthian correspondence; yet it is clear that prophecy was also familiar in other churches.[2] The prophets were recognized as men of pre-eminence in the churches; Paul places them between 'apostles' and 'teachers'

---

[1] I Cor. 12.11.
[2] I Cor. 12–14; cf. Rom. 12.6; I Thess. 5.20.

in a list of types of leadership which God has appointed.[1] Harnack held that this threefold designation of Church leaders antedates Paul, and that the triad, 'apostles, prophets, teachers', represents a type of leadership in Jewish-Christian communities.[2] In any case, prophets do not appear in Paul as authorities in any organizational sense, nor does he say anything about the wandering of prophets from place to place, which appears in Acts and in later Christian descriptions of prophets.[3] As it appears in I Corinthians, prophecy is rather the highest function of inspiration (or gift of the Spirit) for which any 'member' of the body of Christ may hope. In Corinth prophets were familiar and relatively abundant; in fact, any Christian could aspire to be one, even though it was obvious that not all were or would be prophets.[4]

The direction of Paul's discussion of prophecy is determined by the Corinthian pre-occupation with the ecstatic experience of 'speaking with tongues'. This experience was highly prized, and many regarded it as the most striking evidence of the presence of the Spirit. The prophet had direct access to God, and received from God a revelation, which he had to communicate. The message was intelligible; and Paul did not think of the inspiration which brought it as the displacement of the human spirit by the divine, which was a frequent conception in Hellenism.[5] On the contrary, the prophet was in control of himself and responsible to the community for his message.[6] In particular, he must cede to other prophets.[7] Thus prophecy, unlike the ecstasy of 'tongues', was a community matter. Its great value was its ability to 'build up' the church, and in this it showed itself to be an expression of love, rather than of '*gnosis*', though prophecy could exist apart from love.[8] Particularly noteworthy is Paul's advice that when the

[1] I Cor. 12.28.

[2] Harnack, *Mission and Expansion* I, pp. 336 f.

[3] Acts 11.27; *Didachē* xi–xiii.

[4] I Cor. 12.10, 29; 14.1; in I Cor. 11.5 Paul speaks of women 'prophesying'; apparently this is contradicted by I Cor. 14.33–36, though J. Héring, *I Corinthiens, ad. loc.*, holds that the latter passage does not refer to prophesying.

[5] Virgil, *Aeneid* vi.42–76, cited in Guy, *New Testament Prophecy*, p. 132. For the Hellenistic conception of prophecy see also Reitzenstein, *op. cit.*, p. 327.

[6] I Cor. 14.32.

[7] I Cor. 14.29–31.

[8] I Cor. 14.1, 4; cf. Moffatt, *I Corinthians*, p. 216.

prophets speak, the rest of the church is to test what they say.[1]

What the content of such prophecies might be, Paul does not say. It would be a revelation, a direct communication from God.[2] This implies a contrast to 'proclamation' or 'tradition', for the content of these was fixed in advance. Paul suggests two criteria by which to test inspired utterances: one, that the inspiring Spirit must proclaim that 'Jesus is Lord';[3] the other, that the content must upbuild the church.[4] Possibly the content of such prophecies was largely apocalyptic; that is what is to be expected from the apparent origin of Spirit-experiences in the Church, in connexion with the beginning of a new eschatological era.[5] Guy observes that exhortations concerning the imminent end would be considered to 'build up' a church in which the expectation of the end played a large part, and holds that the appearance of prophecy in connexion with a specific eschatological period is probably the reason for Paul's viewing it as a temporary phenomenon.[6] None the less, in view of the apparent sympathies of the Corinthians for Hellenistic gnosis, it cannot be said that the actual content of their prophetic utterances was limited in any specific way.

Thus in the Corinthian situation, at least, prophecy appears as a rather diffuse manifestation of spiritual experience. A prophet was one convinced that God spoke directly to him. Paul praises the 'prophetic' experiences of the Corinthians because they are so manifestly superior to the even more diffuse and individualistic ecstasy of 'speaking with tongues'. The limitations which he set for prophecy were fairly general: a recognition of the lordship of Christ and a recognition of responsibility, exercised in love, to aid in the 'teaching and encouraging' of the community. When Paul makes these points he is shaping prophecy into something more conformed to the 'prophetic' religion of the Hebrew scriptures. It is noteworthy, however, that Paul does not in any way identify the prophets with whom he was familiar with the Old Testament prophets. It was not these specific figures which controlled his conception of the religious experience which he

[1] I Cor. 14.29.
[2] I Cor. 14.30.
[3] I Cor. 12.3.
[4] I Cor. 14.4, 31.
[5] Acts 2.15–21, 33.
[6] Guy, *op. cit.*, pp. 105, 115; cf. I Cor. 13.8.

called prophecy, but rather the Old Testament and Jewish piety in general.

The background of prophecy in the Old Testament and Jewish piety becomes evident if Paul's remarks about prayer are examined. Prayer and prophecy are closely related phenomena, grouped together by Paul.[1] An examination of Paul's conception of prayer shows it to belong to the Hebraic or 'prophetic' type. Friedrich Heiler has shown that, although none of Paul's prayers is preserved in its exact wording, his life of prayer falls into the 'prophetic' type.[2] This means that for Paul prayer is an encounter of personalities, not the absorption of man's personality into God.[3] It means that prayer is thought to change the situation, not merely the suppliant's attitude.[4] It means that the great goal toward which prayer looks forward is the consummation of God's purpose.[5]

Specifically, Paul asks the churches to pray for himself; he wants their prayers for the success of his offering to Jerusalem so that he may come to Rome,[6] for his deliverance from a danger such as he has just escaped,[7] for his own salvation (or deliverance from prison),[8] and generally that his work for the Gospel shall succeed.[9] He suggests that the prayers of the Jerusalem church for the Corinthians are a notable aspect of the fellowship of Christians which also finds expression in the Corinthian gift to be made to Jerusalem,[10] and mentions the prayers of Epaphroditus for the Colossians.[11] Frequently he urges the churches to prayer and

---

[1] I Cor. 11.4–5; 14.13–19.

[2] F. Heiler, *Prayer: A Study in the History and Psychology of Religion*, trans. and ed. by Samuel McComb, Oxford, 1932, ch. 9.

[3] 'The emotions which move the prophetic genius to prayer possess a positive reference to a self; his own or another's ego has to him a worth, or a simultaneous worthiness and unworthiness. . . .' Heiler, *op. cit.*, pp. 230 f.

[4] Heiler, *op. cit.*, p. 279, holds that in 'prophetic' prayer of the New Testament type it is even implied that God's will may be influenced or altered.

[5] *Ibid.*, pp. 248 f.

[6] Rom. 15.30–32.

[7] II Cor. 1.11.

[8] Phil. 1.19.

[9] Col. 4.3; II Thess. 3.1; cf. I Thess. 5.25; cf. Eph. 6.19.

[10] II Cor. 9.14.

[11] Col. 4.12.

thanksgiving.[1] His own prayers in his letters are more general, including usually thanksgiving, and prayer for the steadfastness and increasing faith of his churches.[2] He mentions also his 'heart's desire and prayer to God' for his own people.[3] Of his own personal prayers he tells little, beyond the memorable struggle with the 'thorn in the flesh': 'Three times I besought the Lord about this, that it should leave me; but he said to me, "My grace is sufficient for you, for my power is made perfect in weakness".'[4] Here prayer is the direct request for help in need, as it is in the advice to the Philippians to 'have no anxiety about anything, but in everything by prayer and supplication with thanksgiving let your requests be made known to God.'[5] The eschatological note appears in the traditional exclamation, Maranatha, 'Our Lord, come!'.[6]

Thus though the content of prophecy is not discussed by Paul, the content of the related phenomenon, prayer, is frequently referred to. Prayer is request[7] and thanksgiving. In it the worshipper places his needs before God, and it is expected that God takes seriously the human person and his needs, so that the outcome may be changed by prayer. All this is typical of that Hebrew-Christian type of prayer which Heiler has designated as 'prophetic'.[8]

In Paul prayer is an activity in which personality comes into full realization of its 'polarity' with God. But prayer is not, as Paul conceives it, simply an activity of human personality. The Spirit participates in prayer. Thus the address to God as 'Abba, Father,' is once spoken of as the human appeal to God, once called the outcry of the Spirit.[9] The Spirit 'helps us in our weakness; for we do not know how to pray as we ought, but the Spirit himself intercedes for us with sighs too deep for words.'[10] The language here is similar to that of Hellenistic mysticism, in which the Spirit replaced the human self. But as Lietzmann observes, the similarity in language must not conceal the distinctiveness of the Pauline

[1]Rom. 12.12; I Cor. 7.5; Phil. 4.6; Col. 4.2.
[2]Rom. 1.8–10; I Cor. 1.4; Phil. 1.3, etc.
[3]Rom. 10.1.
[4]II Cor. 12.8–9.
[5]Phil. 4.6.
[6]I Cor. 16.22.
[7]Rom. 10.1, Phil, 4.6, etc.
[8]Heiler, *op. cit.*, p. 251.
[9]Rom. 8.15–16; Gal. 4.6.
[10]Rom. 8.26; cf. v. 27.

conception of Spirit; Paul does not imply that the Spirit substitutes for the personality, for he thinks differently about what the Spirit is.[1] Throughout, Paul assumes the encounter of selves, and assumes the seriousness of the world of events, so that prayer can be concerned with need and with the changing of events.

The discussion of prayer, a phenomenon closely related to prophecy, has shown Paul's conception of prayer to be governed by ideas which spring largely from the 'prophetic' tradition of prayer; and this makes it extremely probable that prophecy also, for Paul, was 'prophetic' in the same sense (though not necessarily for all his Corinthian converts). Prophecy was concerned, that is, with the fate of the community, and it took seriously the encounter of God and man. This is quite in harmony with the criteria for genuine prophecy which Paul establishes, viz., its confession of Christ and its upbuilding of the Church. Paul's conception of prayer and prophecy was 'prophetic', however, in the same sense in which many of the Psalms are prophetic. That is, prophecy and prayer were not for Paul distinctive expressions of the life of the individual who is compelled to come out from the community, and to speak to it in condemnation or leadership on behalf of God. They were rather expressions of the common piety of the community. Prophecy, and even more, prayer, were not the marks of an overpowering individual vocation. Prayer is for all, and any man, and Paul concedes, even women, in the Christian community, may aspire to prophecy, and many will receive this gift.

Thus the prophets of Paul's churches were not assimilated to the Old Testament prophets. The Old Testament prophets are frequently quoted as Scripture, and are mentioned as a class as witnesses to Christ or to God's righteousness.[2] Otherwise the only mention of these prophets as 'prophets' is in connexion with their suffering and martyrdom, which testifies to the disloyalty of God's people.[3] Once the prophets are brought into connexion with Christ in this way: the death of the prophets and of Christ is produced by the same kind of disloyalty to God which is producing the suffering of the Thessalonians.[4] The Old Testament proph-

[1] Lietzmann, *An die Römer*, pp. 86 f.
[2] Rom. 1.2; 3.21; cf. Rom. 16.26, 'prophetic writings', in the doxology appended to Romans.
[3] Rom. 11.3, quoting I Kings 19.10.
[4] I Thess. 2.15.

ets, it is clear, fall into a very different class from the prophets with whom Paul was acquainted. The Old Testament prophet on the one hand had a much sharper awareness of God as distinctively active in historical crises, and on the other, a much stronger conviction of individual vocation. The Pauline prophet was subject to a much more varied inspiration, and judging by the later history of Christian prophets, it was precisely the inability of Christian prophecy to anchor itself securely in the historic witness that led to its eventual discrediting. Later writers speak of Christian prophets believing that they spoke directly for God,[1] and of their position as travelling leaders in the Church; but the distinction between 'prophecy' and 'traditional teaching' grew wider and wider.[2] The simple criteria suggested by Paul were an inadequate control, and the outburst of prophetic enthusiasm under Montanus finally discredited prophecy in the Christian group.[3]

Paul never called himself a prophet directly, though since he affirms that he himself can 'speak with tongues', it is a fair inference that he can also prophesy.[4] He prefers to describe his own activity as 'preaching the gospel' rather than as 'prophesying', because 'preaching the gospel' suggested that the message had a definite kerygmatic content.[5] The Old Testament prophets have played a part in determining Paul's attitude toward his work, but the true successor to the Old Testament prophet is the apostle, and in Paul's writings prophets occupy a much less distinctive place.

MARTYR

The martyr was a figure not unrelated to the prophet. It has been noted above that suffering was for Paul one of the characteristic marks of the canonical prophets,[6] and 'woes' for the righteous play a part in most visions of the final apocalyptic drama. Hence it is

---

[1]Celsus, in Origen, *Contra Celsum* VII.8f., quoted by Lietzmann, *An die Korinther*, p. 68.

[2]*Didachē*, xi-xiii.

[3]Harnack, *op. cit.*, I, pp. 352 f.

[4]I Cor. 14.18; cf. I Cor. 13.9.

[5]'Prophesy', eleven times, never limited to Paul's own activity; 'preach the gospel', seventeen times, of which fourteen refer specifically to Paul's own activity.

[6]See p. 110; cf. Matt. 23.29–31.

necessary to inquire whether Paul had a conception of martyrdom which illuminates his view of man in history.

Within a century of Paul's time the 'martyr' had become a very important figure in the Church. The martyr was one who testified to God by his suffering and death.

For Paul, the understanding of suffering is set in the context of God's purpose for the community as a whole, and the martyr-hero is not an important figure.

As for terminology, Paul does not speak of 'martyrs' in a technical sense, nor does the word *martys* have even the special meaning which it has in Acts, viz., a witness to the resurrection of Christ.[1] With Paul, 'witness' or 'martyr' is a metaphorical term, commonly occurring in a phrase such as 'God is my witness'.[2] The corresponding verb 'testify' and the noun 'testimony' are applied to the authoritative proclamation of the gospel, but these terms may also be used more generally, to mean solemn testimony of any sort.[3] The noun 'testimony' is the nearest to a technical term, usually meaning authoritative testimony to the gospel. It is clear that the special meaning 'martyr' is quite absent from Paul's vocabulary.

None the less, some of the elements of 'martyrdom' are present in Paul's thought.[4] The principal features of the martyr in Judaism and in Christianity were testifying for God and suffering for God. These were united as early as Deutero-Isaiah. Paul also unites the conceptions of witness and suffering. The difficulties which the Thessalonians have encountered have made their testimony effective 'everywhere'.[5] His own imprisonment and even the jealous opposition of some of the brethren have actually advanced the

[1]R. P. Casey, 'Μάρτυς', in *Beginnings* V, pp. 33 f.

[2]It is used once in its literal meaning, 'legal witness', II Cor. 13.1, quoting Deut. 19.15; 'God is my witness', Rom. 1.9; cf. II Cor. 1.23; Phil. 1.8; I Thess. 2.5; 'you are my witnesses, and God also', I Thess. 2.10. Paul never uses the word of himself.

[3]*martyreō*, in reference to the gospel, I Cor. 15.15; other uses, Rom. 3.21; 10.2; Gal. 4.15; Col. 4.13; *martyromai*, in reference to the gospel, I Thess. 2.12; cf. Eph. 4.17; other use, Gal. 5.3; *martyrion*, in reference to the gospel, I Cor. 1.6; 2.1 (in one text); II Thess. 1.10; other use, II Cor. 1.12. *martyria* is not used by Paul.

[4]E. Lohmeyer, 'L'idée du martyre dans le Judaïsme et dans le Christianisme primitif', *RHPR* VII (1927), 316–29; O. Michel, *Prophet und Märtyrer*, Gütersloh, 1932, *passim*; Stauffer, *NT Theology*, pp. 185–8.

[5]I Thess. 1.6–8.

work of proclamation.[1] His task was often carried on 'in the face of great opposition', as his famous lists of trials makes vividly clear.[2]

Lohmeyer has observed that behind the idea of a suffering testimony to truth is a view of two worlds locked in a conflict in which the good cannot be victorious at least until the final end.[3] This dualistic thought is not absent from Paul. He contrasts the suffering righteous with their wicked persecutors, and looks forward to the time when God will grant rest to his chosen and administer destruction to their enemies.[4] On the whole, however, it is fair to say that this commonplace of Jewish apocalyptic appears with striking infrequency in Paul's writings. The reason is that the 'dualism' has already been partially overcome.

Several further points which Paul has in common with the typical martyr-theology may be noted. Suffering is characteristically described as something which comes upon the believer from without, from the evil world, rather than from evil within him, and it is a mark of eschatological conflict.[5] Inner suffering appears most commonly in Paul as a result of his unity with other sufferers or sinners.[6] His commonest comment on the difficulties of life is the advice to 'stand fast', to 'endure'.[7]

Paul likewise mentions the disciplinary or educational value of suffering, though he does not emphasize this.[8] More typical is his view that suffering may be offered to God and that by virtue of it one is united to Christ.[9] In one striking passage he goes so far as to say that he 'completes what remains of Christ's afflictions'.[10] This

---

[1]Phil. 1.14–18.
[2]I Thess. 2.2; cf. II Cor. 11.23–29.
[3]Lohmeyer, *op. cit.*, 318.
[4]Phil. 1.28; II Thess. 1.4–10.
[5]His most common term is *thlipsis* ('affliction'), which was uncommon outside the LXX and New Testament, and was apparently given currency by the need to find a special term for the 'eschatological' suffering associated with the final conflict between God and Evil. Cf. H. Schlier, '*thlibō, thlipsis*', *TWNT*, III, 139–48.
[6]II Cor. 11.28–29; Rom. 9.1–2; but cf. Rom. 7.
[7]'Hardly any word used by the apostle is more characteristic of him than the frequent *stēkete* "stand firm".' M. S. Enslin, *The Ethics of Paul*, New York, 1930, p. 216. Paul uses a number of similar terms, especially *hypomenē, hypomenein*.
[8]Rom. 5.3–5.
[9]Phil. 3.10–11; II Thess. 1.5.
[10]Col. 1.24.

striking thought does not depend on the idea that the Church is the body of Christ and that Christ suffers when it suffers. Neither does Paul refer to a supplement for Christ's suffering on the cross. Rather he refers to the eschatological sufferings associated with the fulfilment of Christ's conquest, and here shows his high eschatological vocation in that he can bear a significant part of these appointed woes.[1] The very intensity of his suffering is a paradoxical sign that evil is being overthrown. Though suffering is an inevitable aspect of the life of any Christian, as he is called to set himself over against the world, Paul takes the depth and persistence of his own difficulties as signs of his special vocation.[2]

That suffering is characteristically brought about (for the faithful) by external evil; that it must be combated courageously; that it has disciplinary value, and that it unites the believer with God (or Christ), are points of similarity between Paul and the typical martyr theology. On the other hand, Paul's thought differs from that of the typical martyr-theology in several ways. Paul did not place any special value on death as the culmination of the sufferings of the faithful.[3] On the contrary, his death, he thinks, will simply mark the end of his effectiveness, so that in spite of his desire to be with Christ, he prefers to live.[4] The attempt to show that Paul found a special eschatological or missionary significance in his death is not convincing.[5]

In the second place, there is little in Paul's conception of suffering as a witness to Christ or as a kind of fellowship with Christ to mark out the 'martyr' as distinctive from the community. While suffering is a mark of the apostle, in whom the tension between this age and the age to come shows itself at its sharpest,[6] Paul regards his suffering as a calling or gift which he shares with all

[1]See C. Masson, *Colossiens* (CNT 10), Paris, 1950, pp. 110–11. Note that here (only) Paul speaks of the 'afflictions' (*thlipseōn*) of Christ, and not of the Cross; contrast with I Cor. 1.13. Cf. G. Kittel, 'Kol. 1, 24', *Zeitschrift für systematische Theologie* XVIII (1941), 186–91, whose association of Col. 1.24 with Jesus' specific words about the suffering of his followers is dubious, though he rightly emphasizes the eschatological understanding of the sufferings of Christ.
[2]Cf. also II Cor. 1.3–7; 11.21–29.
[3]Cf. IV Macc. 6.24–30; Ignatius, *Romans* 1.2, 4; *Mart. Polyc.* xiv.
[4]Phil. 1.19–26.
[5]See pp. 87 f.
[6]II Cor. 1.3–11; 4.7–12.

the Church.[1] This attitude is a marked contrast to the type of thought which tended to isolate and glorify the suffering witness to God's truth. The absence of the tendency to glory in the subjective aspect of his sufferings (a tendency already visible in Ignatius) is a reflection of the completeness with which Paul saw his whole existence, and that of the Church, imbedded in the context of God's decisive action.

In the third place, in Paul the emphasis on the special value of suffering is only incidental. Suffering is expected; it is 'normal'.[2] It has its value. But the 'problem of suffering' is not a problem for Paul. It was not a problem principally because of his conviction that the new age was already in part present. 'Who shall separate us from the love of Christ? . . . in all these things we are more than conquerors through him who loved us.'[3] Thus the dualistic pessimism of the typical martyr-theology is conceded by Paul only in a qualified sense. Suffering continues unabated, but more real than the evil and suffering are the new age and the new life which Christ gives.

As a consequence, Paul did not take a merely passive attitude toward suffering. It was for him an incident in a life of achievement. The new age is not conceived to be one of gradual growth toward perfection, yet it is one in which real achievement is the mark of the obedient life. 'What Christ has done in me', rather than 'what I have suffered for Christ', is the predominant note in his thought.[4]

In summary, Paul's conception of the suffering witness is on the whole not specially related to his view of his own vocation as an apostle; suffering is for all. His view of suffering does, however, illuminate his understanding of the new eschatological situation in which the whole community of Christ finds itself, as well as his view of man's obedience as an active rather than a passive response to the difficulties and hardships of life.

[1] I Thess. 3.3.
[2] *Ibid.*
[3] Rom. 8.35, 37.
[4] Cf. Sanday and Headlam, p. 125.

VII

MAN AND THE MAN

THE principal ways in which Paul thinks of God as working through individual men have been surveyed, and it has been shown that in an abundance of metaphors drawn primarily from Jewish but also from Hellenistic thinking, Paul expresses the conviction that a man may be chosen by God to represent him and act for him. Though for Paul the term 'prophet' is not important in this connexion, the understanding of vocation which he displays is closely paralleled by that of the Hebrew prophets, for, as Paul sees it, man is drawn by his vocation into the transcendent-historical purpose of God, and may even be used to participate in the great change which God is working in human and cosmic existence. Now Paul's view of Christ must be examined, in order to see what relation exists between the activity of God in chosen men, and the activity of God in the Man, Christ Jesus.

The inherited concepts of Jewish eschatology provide the primary framework in which Paul thinks of Christ, though, probably because already incorporated into Jewish apocalyptic, some typically gnostic patterns of thought also appear. Concrete content is given to this framework by Paul's life of faith and that of the Church, behind which stands the figure of Jesus. As John Knox says, 'it is the present living reality which comes first to his mind when he speaks of Christ.'[1]

Paul presents Christ as a pre-existent, heavenly figure, the agent through whom God has begun to establish the new age, through whose entry into human life and identification with man, even to death, a decisive though hidden victory over the powers of evil has been won. As yet the power of Christ's victory is known only by faith within the Church, but the work of God through him in the Church severs the believer radically from the environing power-stucture, and in principle a totally new orientation is given

[1]Knox, *Chapters*, p. 130.

in faith, an orientation which stems from the living presence of the Lord who has overthrown the powers of the world. The human Jesus is accepted as a fact, but receives almost no direct attention except in his death. This emphasis alone suggests that Paul does not regard the life of Jesus as at all parallel to the lives of other men through whom God has acted; and a closer examination of the ways in which Paul speaks of God acting in Christ confirms this impression. To make this clear it will not be necessary to examine the whole range of Paul's thinking about Christ, but only to look at aspects which show, or have been thought to show, parallels to the ways in which Paul thought of God working through other men.

There are three principal ways in which a parallel or similarity may be seen between the presence of God in Christ and his work in other men. First, Christ may be seen as a link between God and man in the creation. Second, parallels may be seen between Christ and certain other men through whom God worked. Third, the Christian life as 'imitation of Christ' may show a similarity in the work of God in Christ and in his imitators. These three possibilities are now to be examined.

CHRIST IN THE CREATION

Paul presents Christ as establishing a new situation in which God and man come together, a new creation. But Christ is also pre-existent, and is associated, in Corinthians and Colossians, with the original creation.[1] How does Paul think of this pre-existent figure—as man, or as divine? Johannes Weiss, whose position has been elaborated by Jean Héring, held that the Pauline Christ belongs in the category 'man'. Christ is, in fact, the 'divine man', the original pattern of mankind.[2] On the other hand, investigators who differ as widely as A. E. J. Rawlinson and William Morgan would agree that Paul's Christ was divine rather than 'Man'.[3]

The point of departure for this discussion is an ancient Near Eastern myth of creation, in which a prototypal 'man', a creation

---

[1] I Cor. 8.6; Col. 1.15-20.

[2] Weiss, II, p. 484; J. Héring, *Le royaume de dieu et sa venue*, Paris, 1937, p. 168; *Die biblischen Grundlagen des christlichen Humanismus*, Zurich, 1946, *passim*.

[3] A. E. J. Rawlinson, *The New Testament Doctrine of the Christ*, London, 1926, pp. 132 f.; William Morgan, *The Religion and Theology of St Paul*, Edinburgh, 1917, p. 56.

of the good gods, is involved in the struggle through which creation emerges out of chaos. In the process a portion of the primal man is imbedded in the creation. Carl Kraeling, who has examined the myth with great care, holds that it is of Iranian origin and in its early stages a cosmogonic myth or interpretation of creation. This 'Anthropos myth' may be used to show that each man has in him an element of life derived from the primal man; and the primal man may be thought of as the model from which created men were patterned. Almost everything that is known about the Anthropos myth or myths comes from gnostic sources of a date later than Paul; the myth played a considerable role in Manichaeanism. In these later forms of the myth a soteriological role is added to the original cosmogonic role of the Anthropos. Man's being consists essentially of an emanation of divinity; the saviour's act then is fundamentally the redeeming of himself. Here emerges with great clarity a typical 'eros' pattern of piety. Whether or not the Anthropos plays a soteriological role, the basic motif of the myth is the hidden kinship between man and the divine. Kraeling holds that the main impact of this myth on Jewish and Christian thought came through its helping to shape the figure of the 'Son of Man' in Daniel and Enoch. He thinks it questionable that Paul himself was directly acquainted with the Anthropos speculation.[1] Weiss and Héring, however, believe that Paul's idea of Christ as the foil of Adam, the 'man from heaven', the figure who 'existed in the form of God', reveals a conception of a divine man which was directly derived from the Anthropos myth.

In Rom. 5, Paul presents Christ as the 'one man' whose act of righteousness constitutes a new humanity, just as Adam's transgression had established a corrupted humanity. Here there is no mention of the creation or of the pre-existence of Christ; the span within which these epoch-making events take place is the historical existence of mankind. The solidarity of mankind is assumed but not analysed, and Adam's transgression is presented as a reminder of the universality of sin, rather than as an explanation of it. Likewise, Christ's obedience is presented as belonging to all the new humanity in a way which is not explained. The old conception that primaeval events must be repeated at the end is in the back-

[1] C. H. Kraeling, *Anthropos and the Son of Man*, New York, 1927, *passim* and esp. pp. 178–80.

ground of the conception of Adam as the 'type', *typos,* of Christ.[1]
Paul, however, is compelled not by the power of the creation myth,
but by the power of the new situation which he uses the myth to
describe. And his attention is turned forward toward the act of
obedience by which the 'many will be made righteous'.[2] Taken
by itself, the passage in Romans does not show any interest
in a pre-existent divine man; it does show how Paul assumed that
an act which would reconstitute humanity would have to be the
act of a man; but the context suggests that Paul here means a man
who had existed historically, and thereby identified himself with
mankind.[3]

A similar presentation of the role of Christ as the founder of a
new humanity occurs in I Cor. 15. Once the thought of the Romans
passage is summarized in passing.[4] Later Paul returns to the contrast between Adam and Christ, and works out its implications in
more detail.[5] The Adam-Christ contrast is subordinate to the
general proposition: the spiritual, *pneumatikon,* which is superior,
follows, in point of time, the *psychikon.* In this passage Christ is
called 'the second man from heaven'. These terms suggest far more
clearly than the simpler language of Romans that Paul may have
been using an old myth which spoke of two 'men' in the creation,
the one the 'heavenly man', the other, copied from him, the 'man
of dust'. In fact, Philo does make just this distinction, which he
bases on a separation of the two creation stories. Gen. 1, recounts
the creation of the heavenly man, while chapter 2 tells of the making
of the physical Adam.[6] Kraeling has concluded, from the lack of
interest in cosmogony, that Paul was unacquainted with or un-
influenced by the Anthropos myth, but it appears that the myth,
coming to him through some Jewish Adam speculation such as
that seen in Philo, has made a contribution to his thought. Yet it
is to be noted that here again Paul has remade the myth to correspond to the new realities as he saw them. His insistence that the

---

[1]Rom. 5.14; cf. Weiss, I, p. 434.

[2]Rom. 5.19. In *Test. Levi* 18.10, if the text is correct, one of the functions
of the Messiah is to 'remove the threatening sword against Adam', i.e., to
undo what Adam had done. Cf. Kraeling, *op. cit.*, p. 175.

[3]Héring, *Christlichen Humanismus,* pp. 8 f., holds that the 'man' here means
the primaeval, heavenly man.

[4]I Cor. 15.21–22.

[5]I Cor. 15.45–49.

[6]Philo, *Leg. Alleg.* i.31–38, 42, 53–55.

'spiritual' man comes last is not improbably polemic against the view that the basic point of contact between man and God is to be found in the original, prototypic man, i.e., in the creation.[1]

The Corinthians passage differs from the Romans section in that there is little explicit reference in it to the 'work' of Christ.[2] He is presented in terms of what he is, not what he does. This fact leads Héring to conclude:

> Here too the Saviour did not first 'become man' by his earthly birth, but he was already man through his heavenly birth. He is a man of divine origin. His descent to earth is necessary for man's salvation, but 'human nature' is not added to him thereby.[3]

Even here, however, the emphasis is clearly on Christ as acting in God's plan of history, not as a pre-existing man. This is shown by the fact that, though little is said specifically about what Christ has done, the whole point of the passage is that the heavenly man comes second, after the earthly.[4] This emphasis is all the more noteworthy because here the 'heavenly man' is described as the one whose 'image' we shall bear; and the 'image' is an element in the creation story. In other words, Paul's attention is fixed on the 'new creation' so strongly that it is difficult to see what assumptions about the original creation he held.

Before investigating the question of the 'image of God' in Paul's thought, one other passage which presents Christ's function must be discussed. This is the famous Christological passage in Philippians.[5] It would be foolish to press this passage for details of Pauline usage, since it is now seen to be a pre-Pauline hymn. None the less, the passage is a central statement of an understanding of Christ's significance which Paul shared. In it, in a gnostic pattern of descent and ascent, it becomes explicit that Christ is a pre-existent figure existing 'in the form of God'.[6] Héring holds that the 'form of God' means the 'image of God', and finds in this passage the classic illustration of the thesis that Christ's humanity was, according to Paul, eternal. Christ existed as 'Man', i.e., the

---

[1]Héring, *Royaume de dieu*, p. 154; Lietzmann, *An die Korinther*, pp. 85 f.
[2]But cf. I Cor. 15.45: '. . . the last Adam became a life-giving Spirit.'
[3]Héring, *Christlichen Humanismus*, p. 8.
[4]Moffatt, *I Corinthians*, p. 263.
[5]Phil. 2.5–11.
[6]Phil. 2.6.

'image of God *kat'exochēn*', and served consequently as the model according to which other men were created. He existed in the image of God, but was not equal to God. On the contrary, he did not strive to make himself equal to God, as did Adam, the other representative man.[1] Instead, he freely consented to live like a man and to die; this constituted his obedience.[2] The reward for this act of obedience was the granting him of the great title *kyrios*—a reminder at once of the exalted position of Christ and of his subordination to him who bestowed it.

A traditional pattern of descent and ascent of a heavenly being lies behind the affirmations of this passage. The emphasis of Paul, however, lies again almost wholly on the action of Christ—it is precisely in the action and not in the 'being' that the 'mind' is to be found which the fellowship is given in Christ. Furthermore, as Paul presents it, the passage does not show any interest in the 'man-likeness' of the pre-existent Christ. Here again, the myth has been reshaped so that it focuses attention on the Incarnation, not the Creation. The point of contact between men and Christ is not that both are 'man' in their essential being, but that in the Church men find and participate in the 'mind' which is revealed by Christ's 'emptying himself'. The one thing which Paul never directly mentions, in Romans, I Corinthians, or Philippians, is that Christ's nature forms a link between man and God at the creation. The creation is always by-passed when Paul deals with the attainment by man of the character or image of God. Christ is related to the creation.

---

[1]Hering, *Christlichen Humanismus*, pp. 11, 30–4. But Rawlinson, *op. cit.*, pp. 134 f., and others hold that equality with God was precisely what Christ did possess and willingly surrendered. With P. Bonnard (*Philippiens* [CNT 10], Paris, 1950, p. 43) we hold that much of the earlier discussion of this point has tried to read more knowledge of Christ's 'nature' out of this passage than it contains. The hymn affirms that Christ *did* have equality with God, but this equality is not analysed.

[2]Why Paul does not state directly that Christ 'became a man' has been considerably discussed. For Héring, of course, he was 'man' already. Weiss holds that Paul avoids saying 'he became a man' because of the close association in his mind between man and 'flesh' (cf. Rom. 8.3). Consequently, Weiss says that Paul 'grazes the later heresy of Docetism'. (Weiss, II, pp. 488–90). More recent discussion would emphasize that the passage does not really concern itself with the nature of Christ's earthly manhood. Cf. E. Käsemann, 'Kritische Analyse von Phil. 2, 5–11', *Zeitschrift für Theologie und Kirche* XLVIII (1950), 335.

His role in creation provides for a continuity between the old and the new, and, like Paul's defence of the Law, represents an assertion of the unity of the act of God. But, so far as the 'God-likeness' of man is concerned, Paul simply ignores the original creation and any implications it may have had for an 'original state of innocence'. Man's existence begins for Paul with Adam's sin, and begins anew with Christ's obedience. The omission of any reference to the creation is not accidental. It reflects the way in which Paul has thoroughly reshaped elements of myth and speculation so that they refer directly to the new creation in Christ.

The same situation is shown when one looks at Paul's use of the idea of the 'image of God'. Paul can speak, like the Old Testament, of man being the 'image of God'.[1] But this is not his usual language; he speaks this way only once, in a discussion of the relation between men and women. Man, he says, is the image and glory of God; woman is the glory of man.[2] At this point he adopts the Old Testament language unreflectively. For Paul, however, it is Christ who is properly the image of God, and man will come in turn to bear the image of Christ as he is transformed by the presence of the Spirit. Thus Christ as the 'image' of God suggests on the one hand that in Christ God's character, otherwise unknown, becomes known. He is the 'image of the invisible God'.[3] On the other hand, the 'image' of God's character is to be impressed on the believer; the likeness will become so profound that Christ will be 'the first-born among many brothers'.[4] The presence of the Spirit is the agency by which the transformation is accomplished, and the change is thought of as already begun. Paul can speak of this process in terms which suggest a transformation of the nature of man, but his interest is firmly fixed on the ethical change which is produced.[5]

[1] I Cor. 11.7.
[2] McCasland notes that woman's relation to God is indirect, through man (cf. also I Cor. 11.3), and that the term 'image' is omitted in reference to woman. Cf. S. V. McCasland, 'The image of God according to Paul', *JBL* LXIX (1950), 85–100.
[3] Col. 1.15; cf. II Cor. 4.4, and McCasland, *op. cit.*, 87.
[4] Rom. 8.29.
[5] II Cor. 3.17–18; Col. 3.9–10. The current tendency of exegesis to deny that Paul was concerned with ethical disposition (cf. Käsemann's summary of exegesis of Phil. 2.5–11, *op. cit.*, p. 315) is right in so far as it stresses Paul's certainty that exhortation or appeal to inner human potentialities was fruit-

Thus, in Paul's characteristic vocabulary, Christ, not man, is the image of God, and men are being created, at last, in Christ's image, in the end of time. Not by looking to the past and to something intrinsic in the nature of man, to some affinity between the divine and the human nature, does Paul base his hope for the transformation into the image of God, but on the historic action of God which has at last culminated in the revelation of the very image of God. By virtue of this revelation men may be transformed into what they have not been as yet.

Paul does not entirely neglect the link between Christ and the creation. He never discusses man's 'original state', though this was a subject of speculation in Judaism. Yet he assumes that man's life is grounded in the creation of God. This 'creation theology' finds rather miscellaneous and unsystematic expression. The 'inner man' struggles with opposing forces, and in Christ this inner man gradually replaces the outer.[1] The 'conscience' approves or disapproves.[2] The possibility of perceiving God in the creation was given to men.[3] These scattered comments are never systematically brought together. The nearest approach to a general statement is the presentation, in Colossians, of Christ's role in creation.[4] Here a 'logos' pattern of thought is applied to Christ—the Creation and sustaining of the whole universe are his functions. Doubtless the creation of man is included. Yet even here Paul does not attempt to find in this 'logos' pattern a clue to the relationship between man and Christ. Rather, the passage is directed toward showing the superiority of Christ to the cosmic forces which he created, while the relationship between Christ and man is brought in only when

---

less; but once a man is given standing within the new community, he must work out the consequences and 'become what he is'.

[1]Rom. 7.22–23; II Cor. 4.16.
[2]Rom. 2.15; the strict limitations of 'conscience' in Paul have been emphasized by C. A. Pierce, *Conscience in the New Testament*, and by Bo Reicke, '*Syneidesis* in Röm. 2, 15', *Theologische Zeitschrift* XII (1956), 157–61.
[3]Rom. 1.19–21. Though Paul does not here present a developed 'natural theology', the passage does affirm real though limited and pervertable knowledge of God; cf. the attack on the traditional use of this passage to support natural theology by H. Bietenhard, 'Gotteserkenntnis der Heiden? Eine Erwägung zu Röm. 1', *Theologische Zeitschrift* XII (1956), 275–88.
[4]Col. 1.15–20.

the new eschatological creation, the Church, appears.[1] The fact that Paul does not ever speak of an original state of perfection or a *'restitutio imaginis'* shows that, for him, likeness to Christ or to God is so closely associated with the new salvation that he can hardly think of any kinship between Christ and mankind in general. Rather, it is precisely this kinship which has to be created, and is created, 'in Christ'. Similarly in discussing food offered to idols, Paul concedes common ground with the Corinthians and acknowledges one creator God and also creation through Christ, yet also here the concluding phrase, 'through whom we exist', probably refers to the newly-created eschatological community, the Church.[2] The relation at creation is necessary but never the focus of interest.

Thus a study of the passages in which Christ appears as 'man' or as the image of God shows a consistent pattern of thought. The cosmological interest of the myths from which this language is derived, an interest that played so large a part in gnosticism, is almost completely ignored. The conception of a pre-existing spiritual man, the image of God, does not serve to demonstrate a fundamental kinship between God and man so that there could be a likeness between what Christ has done and what men do. Rather, the likeness is precisely what must be created, and only when a wholly new situation has arisen can one properly speak of 'spiritual' man, created in the image of God. This series of ideas obviously emphasizes the 'more than human' nature of Christ. Paul's use of the 'primal man' image is not developed to indicate a universal representative humanity in Christ at the original creation. None of his conceptions of Christ approaches the 'prophetic' conception of God's work through men which has been seen to be the characteristic way in which Paul thinks of God as acting through men.

GOD'S ACTION IN CHRIST AND IN OTHER MEN

Next, the possibility of Paul's seeing a parallel between God's action in Christ and his action in other men is to be examined.

[1] Dibelius and Greeven, *An die Kolosser*, pp. 10 f.; James M. Robinson, 'A formal analysis of Col. 1.15–20', *JBL* LXXVI (1957), 270–87. The hymnic character of this passage and the parallels in other 'liturgical kerygmatic texts' indicated by Robinson (278) show that the association of Christ with creation is not a specifically Pauline idea.

[2] I Cor. 8.6.

Here it is to be noted first that the series of terms which Paul applies to chosen men are not, for the most part, applied to Christ. Apostle, prophet, and martyr are terms applied to Christ elsewhere in the New Testament, but Paul does not so use them.[1] It is said elsewhere that Jesus 'preached', but Paul never mentions Jesus as a proclaimer of the gospel.[2] Of all the terms discussed above, used by Paul to describe the human agents chosen by God to do his work, Paul applies only two to Christ: 'slave' and 'servant'. Jesus as 'servant' is the human Jesus, the 'servant to the circumcised', by whose service the promises of God are fulfilled.[3] Here there is an assertion of the effectiveness of Jesus' human life, and there may be present some awareness of God's action through Jesus' work in a concrete social setting. But the real framework of thought is the over-arching plan of God, whose promises are fulfilled. The reference to the consequent spread of the gospel to the Gentiles shows that Paul is thinking of Jesus Christ, as usual, in terms of the function of Christ in the divine purpose.[4]

In the Christological passage in Philippians discussed above, Christ is described as 'slave'.[5] There is something in common between what Paul means by himself as a slave, and Christ as a slave; namely, obedience, and the accomplishment of God's will. One can even see in Phil. 2 a picture of Christ as a representative of God, sent into the world, and given the power to act for God in overcoming the opposition.[6] But Paul did not call this representative an 'apostle', since Christ's task involved the deepest humiliation, while the 'apostle', for all his humiliation and suffering, was given immense dignity and worth by his vocation. There is a real

[1]Jesus as apostle, Heb. 3.1; prophet, Matt. 21.11; 'martyr', Rev. 1.5; cf. I Tim. 6.13.

[2]But cf. Eph. 2.17. For Jesus' activity as 'preaching', cf. Mark 1.14, etc. (and I Peter 3.19); Luke 4.43, etc.

[3]Rom. 15.8; for Christ as 'servant of sin' see also Gal. 2.17, where this term is purely rhetorical.

[4]The translation of *diakonon peritomēs* as 'servant to the circumcised' (RSV, Moffatt) puts more emphasis on the human work of Christ than does the translation 'minister (*or* agent) of (the) circumcision' (RV, Goodspeed, Sanday and Headlam, pp. 397 f.).

[5]Phil. 2.7; see pp. 120 f.

[6]E. L. Allen, 'Representative-Christology in the New Testament', *HTR* XLVI (1953), 161–9.

parallel between Christ and the apostle: both are humbled and then exalted. But for Paul only the 'obedience' side of the paradox is in view as he tries to penetrate the meaning of the descent of the Saviour. Thus the similarity between Christ and the believer is to be seen at the point of obedience, but the context of that obedience is very different, and there is, in Paul's use of the term 'slave' for Christ, no imputation to Christ of that 'prophetic' type of vocation which the term 'slave of Christ' implies.

A very different way of seeing a parallel between Christ and other men was suggested by Wilfred Knox. Certain Pauline passages, he held, reflect a 'divine hero' Christology, which is in some ways similar to Hellenistic ways of thinking about human heroes who had 'become divine'. He saw in Paul's thought a view of Christ as a divine man who attained still higher rank by the life of service which he led, and found in this view a parallel to the Hellenistic conception of the hero who attained divinity by virtue of the service which he rendered to mankind.[1]

The most popular figures of this 'divine hero' type were Hercules, Aesculapius, and Dionysus, while these also served as a pattern for the ideal king. The transfer of the conception to the political area is associated with the figure of Alexander the Great. Thus it comes about that the most thorough statement of the Hellenistic 'theology' of the divine hero is to be found in a comment on Roman politics.[2] The basic idea of the divine-hero thinking was that such heroic figures as Hercules, and such rulers as Alexander, made themselves worthy of attaining divinity by being benefactors of mankind.[3] Wilfred Knox held that this Hellenistic conception of divinity conferred on the specially worthy provides a parallel to the Pauline conception that Christ was the 'man from heaven' who achieved a higher exaltation through his life of humility and service. He also held that the conception of a 'man of divine origin, who attained to godhead' enabled Paul to 'insist on the absolute humanity of Jesus' in the face of the possibility that a conception of Christ in terms of the incarnation of the Logos

[1]Wilfred Knox, 'The divine hero Christology', *HTR* XLI (1948), 229-49. Knox finds the 'divine man' Christology in Paul principally in Rom. 1.3-4; Phil. 2.6-11; Col. 1.15-20. The probably liturgical nature of these passages indicates that the theme Knox studied is not a distinctively Pauline one.
[2]Philo, *Legatio ad Gaium*, 78-114.
[3]Wilfred Knox, *op. cit.*, pp. 231-7.

would dissolve away his manhood.[1] While there is no direct trace of the influence of the Hercules legend in Paul, Knox thought it possible that the 'divine hero' conception applied to a figure like Alexander the Great may have been familiar to him.[2] He found in a comment of Plutarch about Alexander a parallel to Paul's description of Christ's humiliation and exaltation.[3] Alexander did not make Asia 'something to be grasped', but in order to make all mankind one people, he 'fashioned' himself accordingly.[4]

Knox's thorough study has shown a parallel which undoubtedly did impress many Hellenistic hearers of the Christian message; in this sense one may correctly speak of a 'divine hero Christology'. But the setting and motives of the Hellenistic theology were markedly different from those of the preaching of Paul. For the Hellenistic emphasis was on the 'virtue' of the hero, as in the title of Plutarch's treatise, cited above, on Alexander. Elsewhere Plutarch cites Alexander as declaring that '. . . (God) made peculiarly his own the noblest and best of (mankind)'.[5] The attainment of divinity thus falls into the pattern of upward striving. The relationship between performing benefits and attaining divinity was often conceived externally, as is shown by the intense preoccupation with 'fame' which ancient 'heroes' reveal.[6] Furthermore, the benefits rendered are seldom conceived to cut beneath the surface arrangements of life. Horace and Virgil can hope that an Augustus has restored the Golden Age, but their poetry does not carry any real conviction that the fundamental sources from which men draw their life have been transformed.[7] Later Christian apologists like Origen made use of the argument that Christ's divinity may be tested by referring to the beneficial effect which he has had.[8] In an even more sharply Hellenistic vein, Origen presents Jesus as a 'self-made man', in answering Celsus' charge that Jesus had lived in an obscure corner.[9] But in Paul all this is lacking.

[1] *Ibid.*, pp. 248 f.
[2] *Ibid.*, pp. 231, 237.
[3] Phil. 2.6–11.
[4] Plut., *De fort. vel virt. Alex.* 1.8 (330d); cf. Phil. 2.6–7.
[5] Plut., *Vita Alex.* 27.6.
[6] Plut., *Vita Caes.* 32.5; 58.2.
[7] Horace, *Carmen Saeculare*; Virgil, *Eclog.* iv.
[8] Origen, *Contra Celsum*, I 67; II 8.
[9] *Ibid.*, I 29.

He shows no interest in the beneficial effects of the career of Jesus. The only way in which he approaches this kind of argument is in calling attention to the existence of the churches as a sign of the power of Christ.[1] His thinking about Christ is theocentric; Jesus Christ is significant because God was active in him, and continues to be, not because he benefited humanity according to some commonly-accepted standards of what is good. Hence there is no emphasis on the 'virtue' of Jesus. Furthermore the principal field in which the conception of the divine hero existed in a living form was one which did not interest Paul—that of politics. The real connexion between Paul's understanding of Christ and Hellenistic views of the divine hero is that both, different as they are, draw on ancient mythical patterns of humiliation and exaltation.

A third type of parallel between Christ and other men may be seen by observing the role of Christ in the history of salvation. Gottlob Schrenck has observed that for Paul history has four turning-points, and at each of them the decisive change is associated with an individual: Adam, Abraham, Moses, Christ.[2] This type of parallel touches a vital point in Paul's thought, and makes clear both his placing of Christ in an historical pattern and his assumption that decisive changes among men take place through men. Beyond this the parallel cannot be pushed, for in drawing these parallels Paul is not thinking either of how the changes are communicated from the chosen individual to the group, or of the relationship between God and these various individuals.

IMITATION OF CHRIST

Finally, the theme of 'imitation of Christ' must be examined. In Paul's teaching, imitation of Christ is a way of describing the Christian's participation in the same struggle with the old age as Christ engaged in. Christ, not God, is always the object of imitation.[3] Imitation of Christ is always a corollary of the present paradoxical reality of salvation in a world which is externally unchanged; frequently the imitation motif is expressed in a char-

[1] I Thess. 1.2–10.

[2] Schrenck, 'Die Geschichtsanschauung des Paulus', p. 77. Cullmann, *Christ and Time*, p. 138, would 'bracket' the Law (Moses) epoch (Rom. 5.20), and see the real parallels between Adam (sin) and Abraham (promise), and Christ.

[3] But not in Eph. 5.1.

acteristic Pauline combination of indicative and imperative. Of this combination Paul's introduction to the hymn of the Philippians provides an example: 'Have this mind among yourselves, which you have in Christ Jesus.'[1] The same combination is implied in the admonition to bear one another's burdens, and so fulfil the law of Christ.[2] For the law of Christ is not an arbitrary decree of Christ; its authority springs from the fact that he himself followed it. Similarly, Christians are to forgive, as Christ forgave them, to receive one another as brothers, as Christ has received them.[3] The motif of imitation is often present indirectly. For instance, the statement that Christ, though he was rich, for our sakes became poor, is introduced to urge imitation, in the practical matter of giving money.[4] Twice the specific word 'imitators' appears in the injunction to imitate both Christ and Paul himself.[5]

In terms of its content for decision, the imitation of Christ is the imitation of Christ's love, lack of self-concern, humility, and willingness to suffer. The culmination of the theme is in the identification of the believer with the sufferings of Christ.[6] But even this culmination of the imitation theme is not an individualistic identification with or individualistic repetition of the sufferings of Christ. It is an outcome of the union with the death of Christ which in principle is achieved in baptism,[7] and its purpose is not to produce an effect on the individual, but to carry forward the work of proclamation.[8] In it, 'Christ is present in the "ministry" of the proclaimer,'[9] and it is an aspect of the total absorption in God's eschatological purpose which characterizes Paul's understanding of the Christian life.

Théo Preiss has observed the instructive contrast between Paul and Ignatius at this point. Paul's 'mysticism of the imitation of Christ' is set firmly in the historical framework. It is seen as part of an eschatological process, and constitutes part of Paul's obedience.

[1] Phil. 2.5. This translation is preferable to 'which was in Christ Jesus'. Cf. Dibelius, *An die Thessalonicher I, II: An die Philipper*, p. 72.

[2] Gal. 6.2.

[3] Col. 3.13; Rom. 15.7.

[4] II Cor. 8.9.

[5] I Cor. 11.1; I Thess. 1.6.

[6] Phil. 3.10; Col. 1.24.

[7] Rom. 6.4.

[8] See above, pp. 111–15.

[9] R. Bultmann, *Theology of the New Testament* I, London, 1952, p. 304.

In Ignatius, whose language is often very similar to Paul's, the orientation is very different. The imitation is individualistic, and the results are to be in the first instance in Ignatius himself. Hence Ignatius does not, like Paul, prefer to remain alive when faced with the possibility of martyrdom. He is pre-occupied with the imitation of the specific act of death, rather than of the radical obedience of Christ. Paul, however, understood his 'imitation' as a way of presenting Christ, and though it can be described in terms of its moral qualities, these are not derived from general moral principles, but from the decision of Christ. His obedience is directed toward its results.[1]

Imitation of Christ, in Paul's thought, thus does not lead toward any conception of an independent repetition, in the believer, of what God has done in Christ. There is a 'participation' in what God has done and is doing, but the action of God flows from the present, living reality of Christ.[2]

This study of some phases of Paul's thinking about Christ has had mainly negative results. It has shown that Paul usually distinguishes very sharply between the ways in which God works through chosen men, and the way in which he works through Jesus Christ. In other words, the attempt to conceive of Jesus as a 'prophet', which has some basis in other parts of the New Testament, and has been very popular in modern times, is almost wholly foreign to Paul. The 'prophetic' type of experience is characteristic of men chosen by God, but different categories are applied to Christ. Furthermore, an interest in the influence or effect of Jesus is almost wholly lacking in Paul.

The only significant way in which Paul sees a parallel between the working of God in Christ and his working in other men is the derivative activity by which God, through Christ, works in the Church. The ethical disposition of Christ is reproduced in his 'members'; they become like him, and imitate him. Christ works in the Church both to bring it together into a more perfect fellowship, and to make his gospel known to the world. This kind of activity of God through the presence of Christ is not the pre-

[1]T. Preiss, 'La mystique de l'imitation du Christ et de l'unité chez Ignace d'Antioche', *RHPR* XVIII (1938), 197–241.

[2]In Ignatius, the individualistic imitation is pushed so far that Ignatius thinks of himself as a source of salvation for the community. *Ibid.*, p. 212.

rogative of the specially chosen leader. It belongs to all the fellow-ship.[1]

In conclusion, it is of the highest importance for Paul that Jesus was a man, but the work of God in the Man, Christ Jesus, is quite different from God's work in other men. There is a similarity in that both find God's gift of exaltation through their choice of humiliation. Yet, on the one hand, God's work through chosen men is derivative from his work in Christ, and, on the other, Paul shows no interest in the 'self' of Christ except in Christ's aspect of obedience. In striking contrast to his pre-occupation with what it means to his own self to be taken up into God's purpose, in thinking of Christ he concentrates entirely on his function.

[1] J. Knox, *Chapters*, pp. 111–13.

INDEX OF AUTHORS

INDEX OF BIBLICAL REFERENCES

Index of Biblical References

Index of Biblical References

INDEX OF OTHER SOURCES